THE TRUTH ABOUT THE BIBLE

THE TRUTH ABOUT THE BIBLE

by

WILLIAM NEIL

HODDER AND STOUGHTON
LONDON SYDNEY AUCKLAND TORONTO

Contents

THE BIBLE IN THE MODERN WORLD

		Page
1	The Bible in the Seventies	9
2	The Bible in the Schools	16
3	The Bible in the Church	20
4	The Bible and the Scientists	25
5	The Bible and the Critics	31
6	The Authority of the Bible	37

WHAT THE BIBLE PROCLAIMS

7	Belief in God	47
8	The Significance of Jesus	53
9	The People of God	59
10	Belief in Man	65

WHAT THIS MEANS FOR US TODAY

11	Guidelines for Action	73
12	Sources of Power	80
13	How the Bible Helps	87

The Bible in the Modern World

I

The Bible in the Seventies

MANY THINKING PEOPLE are becoming more and more
concerned at the cavalier fashion in which the Bible is
being displaced and reduced in status from the position
it has held in this land since St. Augustine came from
Rome to Canterbury. Protestants are sometimes inclined
to claim that it was the Reformation which made the
Bible the book that guided the policies of our nation and
the thoughts of our people. They would do well to
remember that for a thousand years before that faithful
priests and zealous friars reminded gentle and simple folk
alike of the stories and teachings of the Bible in the days
before reading and writing were skills available to all.
They were aided by local craftsmen, by sculptors and
artists, as is evidenced in carving and painting in cathe-
drals, abbeys and village churches. There never was a
time since Christianity came to these islands when the
teaching of the Bible was not known to all.

It is only in our own day that this is no longer true—
and the nation and our people are correspondingly im-
poverished. One does not need to be a Cassandra to see a
connection between the diminishing prestige of the Bible
and the decline in public and private standards of morality. When our prisons are full to overflowing, when
juvenile delinquency has exceeded all previous records,
when drugs and pornography are peddled openly, even
the most tolerant and optimistic among us must wonder

where it is going to end. Walter Lippmann has spoken of
the need for a new 'public philosophy' to save the
Western world from its collective selfishness and irre-
sponsibility. So far as Britain is concerned such a public
philosophy is ready to hand and has served us well for
centuries. It is contained within the covers of the Bible
which still sells more copies than any other book in the
world—apart from the *Thoughts of Chairman Mao*—but
which appears to be less and less read as the years go
by.

The cause of the present unpopularity of the Bible
must be sought at a deeper level than merely saying that
people had too much of it in childhood or that its atmosphere is that of a bygone age. If the latter argument were
valid we should have to jettison not only the Bible but
Shakespeare, Dante and Homer and indeed anything
that was written earlier than the twentieth century. It is
much more a crisis of belief. When Shakespeare refers to
the sea-coast of Bohemia we accept it as an intriguing slip-
up but it does not affect our appreciation of *The
Winter's Tale* because a small detail of this kind does not
really matter.

But the Bible speaks about God and many are no
longer sure that there is a God. It speaks of life beyond
death and many cannot believe that there is any such
thing. It claims that Jesus of Nazareth was God expressed
in a human personality and many cannot see how he
could have been. These are not trivial matters that do
not affect us. They are vital for our own lives and the life
of our society. And if the Bible is not to be trusted on
major issues like these it is of little comfort or importance
if we are told by archaeologists that Assyrian records
confirm the reliability of the Old Testament historians,
or that Roman inscriptions support details in the account
of St. Paul's travels given in the Acts of the Apostles.

If we are to judge by opinion polls, which are probably
more reliable when a General Election is not involved,
the majority of people in this country still have some

kind of belief in God. It is therefore not that a wave of
atheism has engulfed us but rather that people have lost
the sense of certainty about God which the Bible reflects
on every page. It is not that they do not want to believe
in God but that such belief seems more difficult today
than ever before. The Victorians appear to have had no
doubts about anything, including themselves. We on the
other hand seem to be confused about almost everything.

This is perhaps not surprising. The changes that have
overtaken us since the beginning of the century have
been shattering. Most people would agree that the year
1914 marked the end of an age. Until then it could be
said with some confidence: 'God's in his Heaven, all's
right with the world.' The patriotic fervour which sped
the troops on their way to the Front reflected the view
that once the Kaiser had been taught a short sharp lesson
life in Britain could get back to normal. In the event it
never has. The protracted horror of trench warfare and
the loss of a whole generation of the nation's young man-
hood were traumatic experiences shared by almost every
family in the land. The disenchanted Twenties and the
hungry Thirties rammed home the lesson that the hope of
a 'land fit for heroes to live in' had been a pipe dream.

The war of 1939–45 shook the foundations even more
drastically. The Empire began to disintegrate and
Britain became a second class power. The gas-chambers
of Auschwitz were seen to be a symbol of man's bestiality
and demonstrated the thinness of the veneer of civilisation in the modern world. Since the Second World War
we have lived in an armed camp under the threat of total
annihilation at the press of a button or the even more
terrifying prospect of bacteriological genocide. In the
midst of this has come man's successful venture into outer
space, with a moon-landing as a dummy-run for more
spectacular achievements still to come, yet leaving us
with the uneasy sense that the concern of the two great
world powers to develop their space programmes is military rather than dispassionately scientific.

We have become aware that by the use of pesticides we are upsetting the balance of nature in the countryside, that chemical effluents are poisoning the rivers and that despite smokeless zones the atmosphere in any city becomes daily more polluted by the increasing traffic on the roads. When medical experts warn us of the danger to life inherent in drugs, tobacco and alcohol we feel that somehow these things are within our individual control. Pollution of air, sea and land is, however, an insidious process which the ordinary citizen feels he can do little about.

Poverty has always existed and presumably will always exist. World hunger is on the other hand a phenomenon which is accentuated by the relative affluence of the West, contrasted with the malnutrition and border-line subsistence level of two-thirds of the world's inhabitants. Attempts to redress this blatant wrong are bedevilled by the spectre of the population explosion and gloomy predictions are frequently made of the earth being unable to find space or food for the teeming extra millions.

The cumulative effect of the events of the last fifty years and the magnitude of the present threats to our future has been to shake the confidence of many people that there is any truth in the claim of the Victorian hymn that 'God is working his purpose out, as year succeeds to year'. It seems to be much more likely that we are in the words of a modern writer, merely 'parasites infesting the epidermis of a midge among the planets', at the mercy of blind impersonal forces which we cannot control, or at best here to serve our time until in Thomas Hardy's memorable phrase 'the President of the Immortals has finished his sport' with us.

In earlier times when popes, kings and nobles were guilty of crimes they did penance and acknowledged that they had flouted the authority of God. When a Victorian father ruled his family with a rod of iron he recognised that he himself was subject to authority. Beyond his obligations to the Queen and the lawfully appointed ministers of the Crown was his obedience to his Maker and the laws which He had established for the health and well-being of society.

The Victorians believed that they would be held to account for their actions, if not here then hereafter. They were thus not free to do as they liked. Is it surprising that in the bewilderment and confusion that the last half century has produced in all our minds, as a result of which we have lost the sense of any divine authority to which we are all subject, authority of any kind is called in question? Children dispute the right of parents to tell them what they ought to do, parents dispute the right of teachers to discipline their children, students dispute the right of universities to enforce regulations which they find unacceptable, militant shop stewards and trade union officials dispute the democratic right of the ordinary citizen to demand that he should not be held to ransom until some sectional wage-claim is settled.

When Robert Burns wrote that 'the fear o' hell's a hangman's whip to haud the wretch in order', he was expressing in eighteenth-century idiom the truth that for most of us the possible penalties for breaking the law are an insufficient incentive to good behaviour. This happens only when we feel that there are standards of right and wrong which are none of man's devising but which are ultimate principles inherent in the universe, and rooted in the will of God for the wellbeing and good order of society. It is again not surprising that failure to recognise the authority of God over all life has opened the door to a steep increase in petty theft, business 'fiddles', perjury in the law courts, crimes of violence and a cheapening of human life.

The 'permissive society' has been a mixed blessing. It is an undoubted gain that the cobwebs of Victorian prudishness have been blown away and that children should no longer be fobbed off with stories that babies are delivered into the family in the doctor's little black bag. There is no evidence that the sexual behaviour of the majority of normal young people is much different today from what it has ever been. Promiscuity has not replaced the old-fashioned boy–girl relationship which still leads to marriage, home and children, and the greater availability of contraceptives has decreased the misery attendant on the arrival of an unwanted child.

What is disturbing is not that healthy sex education has been brought into the open but that pornographic films, books and magazines are no longer confined to the sleazy shops and underground cinemas where they belong but are foisted on the general public by unscrupulous commercial interests. Sex-perversions are by definition abnormal, and impressionable children should not be encouraged to think that they are anything else. In this respect the less they know and hear about these things the better. Mercifully there are signs that the present obsession with sex in cinemas and literature will die a natural death through the sheer boredom of the general public.

But a more serious malaise in our present society is the 'I'm all right, Jack' attitude. Everyone with any heart and conscience recognises that there are under-privileged groups in the community—the chronically sick, the disabled, the elderly, the coloured immigrant. Unless we adopt the Nazi attitude and exterminate the physically weak, the politically undesirable, and the racially unacceptable we have certain obligations to them all. What has been depressing of recent years is the increase of collective selfishness on the part of the more powerful trade unions vis-à-vis the weaker unions, or the demands of professional bodies—doctors, academics, school teachers—for a bigger slice of the national cake, irrespective of the inequalities and injustices in our present society. Collective bargaining is desirable and inevitable. But when the national cake is for the time being at least pretty small can we with hand on heart echo the whining plaint of Cain: 'Am I my brother's keeper?'[1] The answer of the Bible is in no doubt.

The present climate of opinion is therefore unpropitious for taking the Bible seriously. For the Bible speaks of the authority of a God to whom we are all subject and answerable for our behaviour. It invites us to co-operate with God in this as in every age for the renewal of society —which always needs renewing. It speaks to chaotic and perplexing times like our own and offers us guidance to extricate ourselves from our difficulties. But how many people nowadays know what the Bible says—or care?

NOTE

[1] Gen. 4: 9

2

The Bible in the Schools

THERE WAS A time not so long ago when it was accepted
that all children in state schools should as part of their
education receive religious instruction, which meant in
effect that they were made aware of the contents of the
Bible. Now, however, there is a widespread movement
among 'progressive' educationists to abolish compulsory
religious education, to make such religious teaching as
remains 'child-centred' rather than 'Bible-centred', and,
in order to save the child from the frightful peril of being
'indoctrinated', to present the Christian faith as one of a
variety of world religions from among which the child is
supposed to be able to choose the one that appeals to him
most—unless he prefers to choose none at all.

It is often argued that religious instruction should be
left to parents or to Sunday Schools. But most parents
nowadays are no more able or willing to teach their
children about the Bible than to teach them mathe-
matics, and most children nowadays do not attend Sunday School. It is therefore, for good or ill, only within the
framework of their day-school education that the generation now growing up will be given any opportunity to
benefit from the wisdom, inspiration and guidance which
the Bible provided for past generations. It would be disastrous if the Bible were to be relegated to the status of a
text-book in the departments of English literature,
studied in the Authorised Version for the beauty of its

language and not for the power of its ideas. It is a sound instinct on the part of most parents and teachers, if we are to judge by public opinion polls, that moves them to discomfit the abolitionists by voting for the retention of compulsory religious instruction whenever they have an opportunity to express their views.

It is the business of the community as a whole, which after all foots the bill for education, to say in broad terms what the character of education should be. If we think of a child's years at school as in the widest sense education for living, there must be some points in each school-week at which the child has his attention drawn to the need to be honest and truthful, compassionate and tolerant, and when he is made aware of the mystery that lies beyond sense and sight. In this awakening of the spirit, in stimulating a sense of responsibility to the community, in inculcating sound standards of behaviour the Bible has always played a vital role.

Part of the reason for the 'anti-Bible' movement in some educational circles is of course that the Bible has been too often badly taught. Clearly no teacher who believes that most of the contents of the Bible are nonsense should ever be asked or allowed to give scripture lessons. If children get the impression that the teacher has his tongue in his cheek, religious instruction will do more harm than good. By the same token a dogmatic teacher who brushes aside honest doubts and critical questions from intelligent teenagers does his subject a grave disservice however good may be his intentions. But these are fringe cases and the vast majority of teachers of the Bible are sensible men and women, convinced of the value of biblical instruction and availing themselves of the assistance which commentaries and modern techniques afford. The days when a Bible lesson consisted of memorising the names and dates of the kings of Israel are mercifully past.

Whatever truth there may be in the charge that the Bible has been too frequently badly taught, and by the wrong people, the answer is not to abolish the Bible from the school curriculum or to substitute for it garbled and superficial treatment of the Koran, the Vedas and the Nine Classics of Confucius. To do justice to Islam, Hinduism or any other of the great world religions we should need to have an expert on each of them on the staff of every grammar school and preferably a practising Muslim, Hindu or Buddhist as the case may be.

Britain is however part of Western civilisation whose roots are in Greece, Rome and Judaea, and not in Mecca, Benares or Peking. Christianity is the only one of the great world religions that has shown itself to be capable of transcending its local origins—a faith which had its beginning in Asia but which has partly for historical reasons but, more important, by the nature of its message struck massive roots in the other four continents as well. We in Britain are therefore, whether we like it or not, inheritors of this particular legacy, born in a country whose laws, institutions, literature and general outlook have been conditioned by the Christian religion, whose impact on our society has its foundations recorded in the Bible. What we need therefore, if we are to be faithful to our heritage, is not less teaching of the Bible in schools but more—and more and better teachers.

It has been a depressingly frequent experience throughout my time as a university teacher of biblical studies to be told by former students of the difficulties they have experienced as teachers of religious education in schools, both in respect of being granted equal status with specialists in other subjects and of getting their proper allocation of time in the school time-table. Like music and art, religious education is all too often squeezed out of the time-table by pressure of examinations and sometimes for less cogent reasons. It seems to depend too often on the whims of headmasters and headmistresses whether the teaching of the Bible is given even its limited space in the weekly school programme or not.

What one had hoped to see after the Second World

War in the light of the 1944 Education Act, which gave religious instruction a statutory place in the school curriculum, was an increasing number of universities through their faculties or departments of theology directing their efforts side by side with those of colleges of education to the provision of highly trained specialists in biblical studies whose expertise would be recognised in any grammar school as being equivalent, financially and status-wise, to that of any other head of department. Instead of that there has been a trend in recent years to replace biblical studies at university level with vaguely defined subjects variously described as religion, religious studies, phenomenology of religion and the like.

Side by side with the training of biblical specialists one had hoped to see an increasing number of arts and science graduates including biblical studies as part of their degree so that teachers of English, history, foreign languages and the sciences could at the same time have been qualified to give intelligent and knowledgeable instruction in the Bible as part of their working week. The salutary effect upon children of finding that their geography mistress or biology master was equally adept at and concerned about religious instruction has been commented on in many educational quarters.

But even where the machinery for the training of properly qualified teachers of scripture has been available, which has not always been the case, the fact remains that the number of students wishing to qualify as full-time or part-time specialists in the Bible has never been comparable to the number wishing to teach subjects such as history, languages and the sciences. This is perhaps not surprising since theology has never been a 'popular' subject. What is disturbing, however, is that of recent years even this small proportion of students has tended to diminish.

3

The Bible in the Church

THE BIBLE HAS its roots in the Church. Without a Jewish Church there would have been no Old Testament and without a Christian Church the New Testament would not have come into being. Conversely the Church finds in the Bible the justification for its existence, the record of its origins and the blueprint for its continuing activities. It goes without saying, therefore, that if the Church fails to insist on the centrality and authority of the Bible in its worship, its preaching and its teaching, its people cannot be blamed if the scriptures come to play less and less part in their lives. Happily this is not yet the case although there are some disquieting signs that it may happen.

Those branches of the Church in this country which have a fixed liturgy—Anglican or Roman Catholic—are safeguarded in that eucharistic services provide regular public reading of gospel and epistle, and other canonical offices have passages from the Bible embedded in them in accordance with a comprehensive lectionary. This not only ensures that regular worshippers are made familiar with a wide range of scripture but also encourages preaching which is Bible-based with particular reference to the prescribed lessons.

All too often, however, even in churches with a fixed liturgy, the sermon tends to be reflections of the preacher on some topical issue with no attempt to relate it to the Bible passages which have been read, or indeed to relate it to the Bible at all. Congregations in those branches of the Church which have no set forms of worship may fare better or worse depending on how much their particular minister is conscious of his responsibility to expound the scriptures and otherwise give the Bible its proper place in the service. At the lowest level a congregation may be fobbed off with a perfunctory reading from the New Testament and a few words of scripture used as a peg on which to hang an address which has obviously been prepared without reference to a text that appears to have been an afterthought.

It would be wrong in this connection not to acknowledge the splendid work of the Bible societies in encouraging private daily Bible reading and it is remarkable in this materialistic age that so many people still find time for regular Bible study. Tribute must also be paid to such organisations for young people as the Crusaders and the Scripture Union which kindle an interest in the Bible that is carried over into adult life. Again on the credit side the revival of biblical studies in the Roman Catholic Church since the Second Vatican Council is a phenomenon whose repercussions cannot be overestimated.

Despite all this no-one could pretend that any sign of a general revival of interest in the Bible is apparent. In some 'progressive' circles the Bible has become almost a dirty word. For the mass of our people it has become an unknown book. It is not so long ago that we were being told that the fault lay in the archaic language of the Authorised Version which was no longer understandable. Now we have modern translations in plenty, above all the magnificent achievements of the New English Bible and the Jerusalem Bible. Statistics of private Bible reading are impossible to come by, apart from those given in the membership figures of the various Bible-reading fellowships, but there is no evidence of a new upsurge of private Bible study among the general public as a result of the new translations and the plethora of up-to-date biblical commentaries.

If we regard the churches as the place above all where the preaching, teaching and study of the Bible are sustained and fostered, we have to recognise that they now touch only a fraction of the population. We have also seen that in the schools the place of the Bible in education is being increasingly questioned. What then of the mass media? We may discount the press in this connection since apart from recording archaeological discoveries which have some bearing on the Bible, such as the finding of the Dead Sea Scrolls, it is not the business of commercial newspapers to handle biblical subjects. Religious weeklies, whose business it certainly is, do their best to keep interest in the Bible alive but their circulation is relatively small.

Religious broadcasting, whether radio or television, is confined within the strait-jacket of the time-factor. Television with its vast viewing public would be an ideal medium for stimulating interest in the Bible, and indeed much useful work has been done in this field over the years both by B.B.C. and I.T.A. But when the total amount of time available for religious programmes in the course of a week is so limited, specifically biblical topics have to take their place among a variety of other items of a generally religious character. One might venture to wonder whether 'open-ended' discussions of religious issues might not more profitably be replaced by 'positive' biblical programmes, but presumably organisers of religious broadcasting have to provide what the public wants as reflected in programme ratings.

It seems to be an inescapable conclusion that while lip-service is still paid to the Bible as a 'good thing' by most people outside the Church and by many within the Church, it somehow or other has come to seem to be irrelevant to the affairs of everyday life. We can explain this in a variety of ways. Some may say, for example, as many middle-aged people do, that an over-strict religious upbringing with compulsory church attendance, Sunday School and Bible Class has killed any interest in the

Bible they ever had. This may be a true reason for loss of interest in the Bible but hardly an argument for its irrelevance. For it would be the claim of most of those who still feel that the Bible is supremely relevant that it is precisely because they were brought up by believing parents, schooled in the Bible by regular attendance at church, Sunday School and Bible Class that it has come to mean so much to them.

Most of us who come into this category would readily admit that in our younger days regular attendance at church was often irksome, that sermons had to be endured rather than listened to, that Bible teaching as it was provided in Sunday School by well-meaning but inexperienced teachers could be extremely dull, and that we may have come through a period or periods when the Church and all that it stood for had no attraction for us. What we should want to acknowledge, however, with humble gratitude is that despite all this the example of a living Christian faith in the home, the influence of a believing fellowship in a congregation, the witness of good men and women however unskilled who obviously felt that the Bible mattered to them, exerted a powerful influence on our adolescent thinking, perhaps unconsciously, which we are now able to recognise.

Another excuse often put forward for neglecting the Bible is that it seems to be so out of touch with the modern world. Every character mentioned in the Bible lived in an age that had never heard of electricity, telephones, television and the motor car, to say nothing of jumbo jets and the computer. Fridges, washing machines, canned and frozen food and all the various gadgets that most of us now take for granted as essential elements of daily life were altogether unknown. Housewives ground their own corn and carried water from the village well. The man of the house tilled his smallholding, minded his sheep, or plied his trade and sold his wares in a booth on the village street. Journeys were made on foot or on donkeys. Social security and a national health service were ideas that were not even dreamt of.

It could be argued that a book that sprang from such circumstances so radically different from our own can have little or nothing to say to us. This would be true if we expected to get from the Bible ready-made answers to the problems that beset our highly complex modern society—inflation, regulation of prices, labour relations, immigration, the Common Market and the rest. But the Bible was not felt to be irrelevant in the highly civilised society of the eighteenth century or in the highly industrialised society of the nineteenth century.

Previous generations turned to the Bible for guidance on the principles on which a healthy community should be based. It did not upset them that the teaching of the Bible came from a bygone age where superficially the conditions of life were different. They recognised that amid all the changes in mankind's way of life the one thing that does not change is human nature. They found in the pages of the Bible men and women who had to come to terms with life as every generation in history has had to do, who shared our hopes and aspirations as well as our anxieties and our fears. Surely men and women who like ourselves had to bring up families and build a home, who knew success and failure, who had to cope with tragedy, illness and death in a world that was as confusing and frightening for them as ours is for us have still something to say to us? But is it not perhaps the case that we can no longer turn to the Bible for guidance because modern science has finally disposed of it?

4

The Bible and the Scientists

IT IS NOW over a century since Darwin's *The Origin of Species* put the scientific cat among the ecclesiastical pigeons by showing that contrary to popular opinion our first ancestors were not Adam and Eve dating from about 4000 B.C., but primitive organisms dating back millions of years which in time developed into animals and finally into human beings. Except in some odd corners of the globe and among some freak religious sects it is now recognised that the theory of evolution provides the correct explanation of the beginning of human life on this planet and that the violent reaction of religious orthodoxy against it last century was based on a misunderstanding of the nature of the stories at the beginning of the Bible.

We now realise that these stories in the early chapters of Genesis are not intended to teach science but theology. When Jesus wanted to convey some important religious truth to his audience, as often as not he did so in the form of a story which would arouse interest and linger in the listener's mind. Thus in the well-known stories of the Prodigal Son and the Good Samaritan he invented imaginary people in imaginary situations to illustrate his point. He could have spoken at length of the love of God for his wayward children. But instead he drew a vivid word-picture of the joy of an old father at the safe homecoming of his erring son.[1] Likewise Jesus could have de-

livered a homily on helping our neighbours, instead of
which he pictured the different reactions of three types of
men to a wounded traveller lying at the side of the road.[2]

This is the clue to the real nature of the stories at the
beginning of the Bible. The word Adam in Hebrew
means 'man'—not a particular man or even the first
man—and the word Eve means 'life', since woman brings
new life into the world. In describing Eve's creation out
of one of Adam's ribs the Bible is obviously not teaching
biology but expressing the closeness of the man–woman
relationship pointing forward to marriage as its fulfilment.[3] Similarly when the Lord moulds Adam out of clay
and breathes life into him it is a memorable way of expressing both man's kinship with nature and the animal
kingdom, and his dependence like the rest of creation on
the sovereign power of God.[4]

In the story of the Flood[5] we are not being asked to
believe that at some point in time our planet disappeared
under water, nor is our credulity being stretched into
accepting Noah's Ark as anything other than fantasy.
The Flood is the symbol of the judgement of God on the
corruption of the world—today or at any other time—
from which we are only saved by the mercy of God and
for the sake of even one just man like Noah. Nor are we
asked to accept the story of the Tower of Babel[6] as a
scientific account of the origin of different languages. It is
a vivid way of saying that when men in their pride try to
make themselves equal with God the result is confusion
and disharmony, of which the variety of languages is a
symbol.

Once we recognise that there are various ways of
approaching and expressing truth we shall not fall into
the error of trying to reconcile scientific truth with religious truth which was never intended to be scientific.
The stories of Adam and Eve, Cain and Abel, Noah and
his Ark and indeed all that is contained in the early
chapters of Genesis were not included in the Bible by
simple-minded desert nomads but by highly sophisticated

Jewish scholars who knew as well as we do that there was no talking serpent in a magical Garden of Eden,[7] but who also knew how to use ancient myths and folk-tales to convey truths about God and ourselves from which we can still profit.

When we pass from these first chapters of Genesis, which form a prologue to the whole Bible, to the more or less historical record of the fortunes and misfortunes of the Hebrew people, we find inevitably elements which are not historical but legendary and unscientific. This should not put us off since we find legends in all religions, including those associated with Christian saints, like St. Columba or St. Francis of Assisi. We now recognise that the Bible is not asking us seriously to believe that Balaam had a talking ass,[8] that Moses waved his wand and divided the Red Sea,[9] that Elijah went up to heaven in a chariot of fire[10] or that Elisha made an axe-head float.[11] Pious tales of this kind grow up round the memory of holy men in all ages and in all societies. Their chief value is to indicate the impact these men must have made upon their times. Such legends do not arise in connection with mediocrities.

The story of Jonah in the whale's belly is neither myth nor legend but sheer fiction—and very funny. It is sad that the unknown author's joke has so often fallen flat when evidence has been solemnly sought to prove that whales exist with gullets wide enough to swallow a man. How it was hoped to produce scientific evidence that Jonah could compose a psalm while inside the fish is even less easy to understand. The tragic consequences of this misguided attempt to show that the Bible is after all scientifically respectable are of course not only that the author's joke misfired but that his real message behind the fun which is a moving plea for tolerance, charity and mercy was lost sight of.[12]

When we turn to the New Testament and ask the question whether science has undermined its credibility the answer is more complicated. In the last resort the

New Testament would not have come into existence unless a small group of Jews, disciples of Jesus of Nazareth, had become convinced that their Master who had been crucified and laid in a tomb had defeated death and had risen from the grave. The heart of the message which was preached first to Jews and then to Gentiles before being embodied in written form in the gospels and letters of the New Testament was that a unique event had taken place which had profound consequences for the life of the world.

Science can neither prove nor disprove the Resurrection of Christ any more than it can prove or disprove the existence of God or that he created the universe. On the evidence in all three cases it could be said that they are equally reasonable probabilities. Many of us would feel that the same could be said of the evidence that Jesus' birth was unique and that any scientific findings on the subject of parthenogenesis in the animal kingdom are irrelevant. It may be freely admitted, however, that the New Testament evidence for the Virgin Birth of Jesus is less conclusive than the evidence for his Resurrection.

Scientific investigation of the miracles of Jesus as recorded in the gospels is of course perfectly legitimate and here there are bound to be differences of opinion. There was a time when theologians based their claim that Jesus was God incarnate largely on the mighty works that are attributed to him in the gospels. There was also a time when the majority of scientists ruled out the miracles of Jesus as a violation of natural law. There is less dogmatism on both sides today. Churchmen tend to view the miracles of Jesus less as interruptions of the natural order and more as visible signs of the power and presence of God in the world, while scientists are less sure that we know all that there is to be known about the 'laws of nature'.

We know too little of the effect of mind upon matter, and too much about psychosomatic medicine to dismiss out of hand the record of the healing power of Jesus over the mentally disturbed and the physically sick. The fact that all disease in New Testament times was attributed to demon possession does not alter the unswerving testimony of the gospels to the fact that cures took place. If Jesus had lived at some other point in history where mental and physical illness were not attributed to the malevolent influence of evil spirits, the restoration of wholeness of mind and body would doubtless still have been effected.

It would be foolish to maintain that every miracle-story in the gospels and in the Acts of the Apostles is a factual record of what precisely happened. We must allow for the possibility of occasional exaggeration or misunderstanding and no doubt some of the stories have grown in the telling. By the time the gospels came to be written, theological interpretation had become so interwoven with the historical basis that it is often difficult to tell which is which. Some of the stories are so clearly theological in character—like the Feeding of the Multitude[13] and the Changing of Water into Wine[14]—that they are not to be regarded as miracles at all.

A new red herring has recently been dragged into the arena with man's exploration of outer space. Some people felt that this sounded the death-knell of God since the cosmonauts found no trace of him 'up there' or 'out there' as the Bible had taught us to think of him. The biblical view of the structure of the world was that of a three-tier system, with heaven above the earth and hell below it. But even before Copernicus, thoughtful people had ceased to regard the sky as literally the dwelling place of God. They continued to speak of God as being 'up there' because it is the simplest way of expressing the idea of his transcendence.

As science expanded our conception of the universe the phrase: 'God is up there' tended to be replaced by the phrase: 'God is out there', beyond the limits of scientific investigation. But now we know that there are no areas in the whole universe which are not accessible to exploration by man or his inventions. Many people have therefore felt that if God is not 'in the beyond' he is nowhere at all. New ways of describing God have been sought in such terms as that he is 'Ultimate Reality' or the 'Ground of our being'.

Biblical language about God is, however, never scientific but theological. Both the Old Testament and New Testament writers are unashamedly anthropomorphic in their imagery of God. They use symbols and metaphors like poets and painters to convey their conviction that God is everywhere and in every thing—within us, beside us, around us, beyond us, above us. The advent of the space-age has made no difference to the conception of God which St. Paul expressed in his speech to the philosophers of Athens: 'In him we live and move and have our being.'[15]

NOTES

[1] Luke 15: 11 ff.
[2] Luke 10: 30 ff.
[3] Gen. 2: 21 ff.
[4] Gen. 2: 7
[5] Gen. 6–9
[6] Gen. 11: 1 ff.
[7] Gen. 3: 1 ff.
[8] Num. 22: 22 ff.
[9] Exod. 14: 15 ff.
[10] 2 Kings 2: 11
[11] 2 Kings 6: 6
[12] Jonah 1–4
[13] Mark 6: 30 ff.
[14] John 2: 1 ff.
[15] Acts 17: 28

5

The Bible and the Critics

THE BIBLE IS not in conflict with science nor need it be
reconciled with it since like poetry and fine art it uses a
different medium to communicate truth. That is not to
say, however, that scientific methods should not be used
in examining the biblical documents. This has indeed
been done, particularly over the last century and a half,
and it is due to the patient scientific examination of
ancient manuscripts by biblical scholars of many nations
that we have in such modern translations as the New
English Bible and the Jerusalem Bible versions of the
scriptures on whose accuracy we can rely.

Scientific methods have also been used to good effect in
the field of literary and historical criticism of the Bible
from the nineteenth century onwards. It is as a result of
this that we now have a much better understanding of
how the Old Testament was gradually built up over a
period of a thousand years. From the dim beginnings of
the Hebrew people when like any other tribal society
they depended on minstrels and story-tellers before the
days of writing, bit by bit a national literature developed
—poetry, history, law, prophecy—which eventually con-
stituted the Old Testament as we know it.

In the course of their study of the Old Testament,
scholars have solved many of the problems that at one
time perplexed readers of the Bible—contradictions, dis-
crepancies, inconsistencies and the like. They have also

taught us how the Hebrew mind worked in a pre-scientific age, so that we can now mostly distinguish the difference between what is myth and legend and what is factual history. In this they have been vastly helped by the results of archaeological investigation throughout the whole of the ancient Near East, shedding new light on many puzzling features of the biblical story.

Our understanding of the New Testament has been likewise enhanced by responsible scientific criticism of the gospels, showing how and why they came to be written and distinguishing the different approach of the four evangelists to the story of Jesus. The chance discovery of the Dead Sea Scrolls has added much to our knowledge of the religious background of Palestine at the time when Christianity emerged, and the assistance of nuclear physics has even been sought to determine the age of the scrolls themselves. Recently the computer has been resorted to in order to establish whether the letters in the New Testament generally attributed to St. Paul were written by him or not.

Scientific skills and scientific methods have thus been employed by biblical scholars in the conviction that nothing but good can come from free and open enquiry into the contents of the Bible, unhampered by dogmatic considerations or fear of the consequences. It may transpire, as has often happened, that some conclusion reached by a particular scholar is subsequently proved to have been false. This occurs in all branches of study, not least in science. It is by open discussion at meetings of learned societies, by the ventilation of new ideas in journals and books and the critical comments that this provokes from other workers in the same field that eventually a general consensus of opinion is reached and new knowledge filters through to the general public. In the realm of biblical studies this is the normal procedure and over the years it has proved its worth. As the Bible itself puts it: Great is truth and it gets the upper hand.[1]

While this is so, the mass media, in particular the

popular press, have provided a new hazard. It is difficult for the ordinary citizen to distinguish between well-informed biblical scholarship and wild speculation. But from the point of view of competitive journalism religious scholarship is not news whereas speculation, especially if it upsets conventional thinking, undoubtedly is. Thus if reputable scholars advance the view, as has recently been the case, that Jesus may have been a married man or a homosexual, and if these views are widely publicised, it is not easy for the ordinary citizen to realise that this is pure conjecture, based on little or no evidence.

When Hugh Schonfield, an extremely able—and personally likeable—Jew, advanced the theory in his 'Passover Plot' that Jesus had engineered his own crucifixion and skilfully stage-managed a bogus 'resurrection' which did not come off, this was 'news'. Most people who got the backwash of this in the press without reading the book were unaware that Schonfield himself in complete honesty underlined the element of speculation and conjecture in his thesis.

On the occasion of the exhibition a few years ago in various centres up and down the country of fragments of the Dead Sea Scrolls, John Allegro, who had himself been much involved in this field of study, took the opportunity in a spate of newspaper articles to suggest that there was nothing in early Christianity which had not been borrowed from the Dead Sea sect. Again this was speculation based on a minimum of evidence and it was at once publicly discounted by the foremost Old Testament scholars in Britain. Allegro's recent publication *The Sacred Mushroom and the Cross*, which traced Christian belief back to phallic symbolism was equally trenchantly denounced as sheer fantasy by responsible biblical scholars. But popular opinion was undoubtedly influenced against traditional views by the publicity which was given to this wildly improbable hypothesis.

In matters of this kind we can wisely be guided by

science. A scientist advances a theory, which is treated by his colleagues as that and no more. It is one man's opinion and not by any means finally conclusive. In the field of science, however, new hypotheses are Aunt Sallies put up to be knocked down. In the field of religion people can be hurt. Their beliefs can be undermined, and after all beliefs are what people live by. Anyone writing responsibly on matters of religion nowadays must have regard to the effect his views will have on a public schooled by the mass media to think that what the 'experts' say must be right.

We need not be greatly concerned—as indeed the indifference of the British public has confirmed—by the recent controversy in the United States regarding the 'Death of God'. There is a wholesome element of commonsense in this country which dismisses the phrase itself as a contradiction in terms. If there is—or was—a God, how can he suddenly be dead? Most of the American advocates of this misleading nonsense are, perhaps rightly, campaigning against wrong pictures of God. We are certainly well rid of the 'Old Man in the Sky'—if anybody ever indeed thought in this way.

I am more concerned, however, with the Bible and what it has to say to us. And here—and I say this as a product of the Reformation, like most people in this country—I feel that we must take more account of the tradition of the Church. It may have been an obscurantist attitude stemming from the Vatican which forbade uninhibited enquiry into the biblical documents, but at least Roman Catholics were saved from the extravagances of liberal Protestantism. Perhaps now with the remarkable upsurge of biblical studies in the Roman Catholic Church we are beginning to find the way to a new basis of understanding. Why should it not be through the Bible?

As I read the erudite contributions of the German-speaking theological world—with their adventurous exploration of new avenues of thought—I wonder whether

Protestant individualism has not lost something by being
no longer anchored to tradition. The Christian Church
has after all been going on for a long time – almost two
thousand years. It did not start with a New Testament.
The New Testament came into existence because the
Church was already there. Are Catholics not right to insist that we cannot look at the Bible in isolation, that
we must look at both Bible and Church together?

Before a word of the four gospels in the New Testament had been written down the young Christian
Church through its missionaries was proclaiming its faith
that a new age had dawned, that God had disclosed the
truth about himself and his purpose for the world in the
life, death and resurrection of Jesus of Nazareth. These
first missionaries were of course Jews, like Jesus himself,
and although most of their countrymen did not share
their view that Jesus was the long promised and eagerly
awaited Messiah of Old Testament psalm and prophecy,
the missionaries found a ready response for their message
among the peoples of the pagan world.

As we read the story in the Acts of the Apostles of the
first thirty years of the Church's history, together with St.
Paul's letters, it is clear that the words of the Apostles'
Creed which enshrined the faith of the Church in the
second century, are a more precise expression of the beliefs of the first missionary apostles themselves. From the
beginning the Church confessed its faith that Jesus Christ
is Lord and bracketed him with God himself. This faith
was shared by the men who wrote the gospels. We need
not look here for a story of a wise teacher or a social or
religious reformer, but of a mysterious and enigmatic
personality who defies definition in ordinary terms. The
gospel writers see Jesus as the carpenter of Nazareth
indeed, but also as someone who in some strange way
gave those he encountered the sense that they were in the
presence of God.

It has been powerfully argued in recent years, particularly by continental New Testament scholars, that we can

know little or nothing of the actual life and teaching of Jesus but only of the faith of the Church, which is said to be reflected in myths like that of the Virgin Birth, the Resurrection and the miracle-stories of the gospels in general. We are told that once we have 'demythologised' the gospel records we come to the heart of the gospel message, which is our encounter with God through Christ, although in the process Jesus as a historical person has more or less disappeared.

But if we are to be guided by the tradition of the Church and its faith as expressed in its creeds, how could that faith have arisen at all unless Jesus had said and done the extraordinary things that are reported of him in the gospels? It is surely more scientific to say, in the light of the impact which Jesus of Nazareth has made on the world, and on the lives of countless men and women throughout the centuries, that there is a reasonable probability that the picture which the gospels give of a Person who was unique is in fact true.

NOTE

[1] 1 Esdras 4: 41

6

The Authority of the Bible

IT IS NOT surprising in view of recent criticism of the
Bible both from outside and from inside the Church that
many people have already come to the conclusion that
the Bible has lost for ever the authority it once had.
Others are frankly puzzled. They are looking for something to hold on to, a guide to life in troubled times.
Fewer and fewer seem to find their anchor in the worship
of the Church. The Bible might provide such an anchor
but can it any longer be relied on, has its image not become too badly tarnished?

Let us however be clear in our minds as to what kind
of authority we are looking for. There was a time when
the Bible was held to be an infallible handbook to the
whole field of human knowledge. If geologists, biologists,
geographers and astronomers advanced theories which
conflicted with the plain words of the Bible they were
accused of undermining the authority of the Word of
God. The bitter battle between science and 'religion' last
century ended very properly in victory for the scientists.
The Church had invested the Bible with an authority
that was quite bogus.

Nor have the results been any happier when the Bible
has been treated as infallible in all moral and religious
questions. Witch-burning, torture of heretics and the in-
stitution of slavery have been defended on the authority

of the Bible, and in our own day apartheid is held by
some to be in accordance with the purpose of God,
plainly set out in Holy Scripture.[1] As we know only too
well, the devil can quote scripture to his purpose, and no-
one could deny that much cruelty has been practised, and
much human misery has been caused by taking biblical
passages out of their context and treating them as divine
commands.

The Bible cannot be infallible because it was written
by fallible men. They glimpsed some aspects of the truth
about God but not all the truth. Some of them saw more
deeply than others into the heart of the mystery that surrounds us, but they were all men of their times, limited
by the state of knowledge in their own small country in
the particular century in which they lived. Moreover, in
the course of their history the people of the Bible came to
understand more and more about God's nature and purpose, and about the kind of behaviour he expects from
us. There is thus a world of difference between St. Paul's
words on these matters and some of the words attributed
to Old Testament patriarchs, kings and prophets.

If the authority of the Bible does not depend on its
infallibility, does it perhaps depend on its inspiration?
We can no longer accept the view which was held at one
time that the Bible is 'inspired' in the sense that its
writers simply held their pens in their hands and the
Holy Spirit did the rest. This is manifestly absurd not
only in the light of the contradictions and inconsistencies
which we find in the Bible but also because the biblical
writers are obviously, on the evidence of their writings, as
varied a collection of individualists as we could find in
any literature. They were clearly not automata.

But were the writers of the Bible 'inspired' in a different way from, say, Shakespeare, Beethoven and Michel-
angelo? It would be difficult to argue that they were.
Some of them, we should have to say, were a good deal
less inspired than these great masters or even than some

post-biblical Christian writers. If we mean by inspiration that a writer, composer or painter conveys to us through his work something of the ultimate truth and beauty which is in God and comes from God, we can hardly call 'inspired' the detailed regulations for animal sacrifice in the Mosaic law, or the elaborate instructions for the construction and furnishing of Solomon's Temple, to say nothing of some of the more bloodthirsty passages in the psalms or in the chronicles of the kings of Israel. We can if we like say that as a whole the scriptures are inspired, though some parts are more inspired than others, but it seems wiser in talking about the Bible not to use the word inspiration at all.

What word, then, which is still meaningful, can we use in our quest for the authority of the Bible since neither 'infallibility' nor 'inspiration' seems to be of much help. The Bible itself supplies us with the word 'revelation', meaning God's disclosure of the truth about himself and us and the world we live in. The authority of the Bible consists in the fact that it contains this revelation, and it is important to stress that the initiative has come from God. It is also important not to think of God's revelation of himself as recorded in the scriptures as being like the opening of the shutter of a camera, so that bit by bit more light was let through until eventually the whole scene was illuminated.

For the obverse of God's revelation of the truth is man's understanding of the truth. They are two sides of the same coin. It is not as if God grudgingly disclosed certain aspects of himself and his purpose and deliberately left mankind in ignorance until it suited his purpose. The story of the Bible is the story of man's increasing recognition of the inadequacy of his ideas about God. But he is not wresting this truth from an unwilling God. He understands only because God enables him to understand. Hence the Bible emphasises God's quest for man rather than man's quest for God. But the two things are inseparable. God speaks to man but man must be ready to listen.

God has spoken to man in many ways and he still speaks. He has revealed something of the truth about life and the world we live in to poets, painters, philosophers, writers and scientists in all nations and in all ages. Some men at some stages in history have been more responsive, more open to illumination, than the rest—men of the calibre of Homer and Plato and the founders of the great world religions, Zoroaster, the Buddha, Confucius, Muhammad. All of these have apprehended something of the divine mind which orders the universe, something of the purpose which directs the lives of men and nations, something of the nature of the Supreme Being in whom is grounded all beauty, goodness and truth.

But God has chosen to reveal his nature and purpose in a special way in the history of one particular people, the Hebrews, culminating in the fullest disclosure of himself to men in the life of one particular Hebrew, Jesus of Nazareth. It is in the light of this that all our knowledge of God must be judged, all religions and philosophies, all ethical systems, all estimates of what is true and good and beautiful, all guesses as to the meaning and purpose of life. The authority of the Bible lies in the fact that it is the record of this special revelation and that from the first chapter to the last it directs our thoughts to Christ as the clue to the mystery of our existence.

It would be agreed by most thoughtful people that Jesus of Nazareth is a unique figure in world history. Whatever reservations we may have about certain features of the gospel story we cannot ignore the impact Christ has made on civilisation over the last two thousand years, both on the lives of individual men and women and on the character of society itself. However much institutional Christianity may have dragged its feet, however obscurantist the Church may at times have been, whatever crimes and follies may have been committed by professing servants of Christ, the fact remains that when we add up all that has been achieved for the betterment of the life of mankind by men and women who have been committed to Christ's service we must say that no other person in human history has had a comparable effect.

Whether we think in terms of social and humanitarian reform, or educational advance, or organised care for the sick and aged, or concern for the underprivileged and victims of misfortune, the original inspiration of those who have sought throughout the centuries to bring light into men's darkness, turn their despair into hope and make them feel that someone cares, can be traced back directly or indirectly to the words and deeds of Jesus and his continuing influence on the minds of men. What gives the Bible its authority for us today is therefore that it still tells us all that we can know of the man Jesus, of the impact he made upon those who were in a position to know him best, and of the launching of the movement which he founded, which has become the faith that has changed the lives of countless millions in all parts of the world.

It may, however, be said that this certainly gives the New Testament an authority which is shared by no other religious writings. But what of the remaining two-thirds of the Bible, the sacred scriptures of the Hebrews contained in the Old Testament? The answer is that the Bible is one book and that we cannot understand the record of the man Jesus without steeping ourselves in the history and tradition of the people into which he was born and the faith which he inherited. Jesus was not a twentieth-century European but a first-century Jew. Behind him were another twenty centuries of the life and thought of a nation which is itself unique.

No-one has ever found an answer to the question of why God should have chosen the Hebrews to be the channel through which he would communicate the truth about the meaning of life to the world. Why not the Greeks, the Romans, the Assyrians, the Babylonians—all of them more civilised, more powerful, more wealthy? 'How odd of God, to choose the Jews.' Yet he did select this tiny nation on the Mediterranean seaboard, which only for a short time in its long history had any military, political or economic significance, to be his 'peculiar people'. For the Jews are indeed a unique people. After four thousand years of oppression by the great powers of the ancient world and the modern world, they still, as Dean Inge said, live to 'stand over the graves of their persecutors'.

But it is not the fact that the Old Testament is the record of this unique people that gives it its authority for us. Indeed that candid record shows them as a whole to have been little different from any other people in their religious apprehension and standards of behaviour. But from their midst there arose a long line of spokesmen on behalf of God—the prophets of Israel—Moses, Amos, Isaiah, Jeremiah and the rest—who have left a unique legacy of insights into the nature and purpose of God, and the nature and purpose of life. All of them point forward to Christ. The promises made by God through them find their fulfilment in Jesus. The authority of the Old Testament for us today is therefore, as Luther said, that it is the swaddling clothes of Christ and the manger in which he was laid.

We should not expect to find in every chapter of the Old Testament words which speak of Christ. There are arid stretches of the Old Testament which are of interest only to Jewish and Christian scholars. They have little or nothing to say to the average reader of the Bible today. There are also passages which fall far short of the highest insights of the Old Testament itself, to say nothing of the mind of Christ. But they are all parts of the same story of God's plan for the renewal of the life of the world through Christ. In the light of this the authority of the whole Bible is that it is the record of a unique Person, whose coming was prepared for by the revelation of a unique faith to a succession of men whose hearts and minds were uniquely made ready to respond. There is nothing comparable with this in any other religious writings anywhere.

NOTE

[1] Gen. 9: 20 ff.

What the Bible Proclaims

7

Belief in God

IT WOULD SEEM that as far back as we can trace man's existence on this planet as a thinking animal he has never been without some kind of belief in a power or powers beyond himself which influence his life and control his fate. Whether it was expressed in an eerie sense of the uncanny, by the cult of 'high gods among low races', or in the basic concern for food and fertility and the need to propitiate whatever powers were reckoned to provide these, primitive man appears to have felt himself dependent on mysterious forces outside of himself. At a later stage in his development these vague beliefs were crystallised into worship of a wide ranging variety of gods and goddesses, each with a special field of interest and each requiring appropriate offerings of thanksgiving or supplication.

It was this latter type of belief which prevailed throughout the ancient world in biblical times as we know from the myths and legends of Greece and Rome, and from what archaeologists have discovered in the civilisations of the Near East of which the Hebrews formed a part. It was a world in which every city boasted of its piety in a multiplicity of temples and shrines, of altars and images, dedicated to countless deities both native and imported. St. Paul in his letter to the Christians at Corinth speaks of these many 'gods' and many 'lords', and goes on to say 'yet for us there is one God, the

Father, from whom all being comes, towards whom we move'.[1] Where did this belief come from? We find the answer in the Old Testament.

Surrounded by peoples who worshipped the sun, the moon and the stars as gods, the Hebrews worshipped a God who, they claimed, had created sun, moon and stars and all living things. While their neighbours represented their gods in countless images of wood, stone and metal, the Hebrews were forbidden to make any such models of a Being who was so different from anything else in human experience that he could not be depicted in any shape or form. Unlike many of their more civilised contemporaries who painted and sculptured their gods in the form of animals, the Hebrews never spoke of their God except in terms of human personality, the highest terms they knew. And God was always 'He' and not 'She', not out of a conviction of male dominance, but because the female element in other religions led to the temples of the goddesses becoming little more than brothels.

To this day the Jews confess their faith that 'the Lord our God is one Lord' as they have done since Old Testament times.[2] Jesus as a devout Jew confirmed this faith as his own[3] and St. Paul like the rest of the early Christians made it the foundation of his thinking. This conviction that there is but one God is so deeply embedded in Christian teaching that it is difficult not to take for granted that it has always been accepted. Yet the evidence, archaeological and literary, points to the fact that this faith of the Hebrews expressed in the Old Testament was no evolutionary development from more primitive beliefs but a radical break with all previous thinking about God.

The Hebrew word for God was YHWH, probably pronounced Yahweh and more familiar to us in the form Jehovah. Normally it was, however, not pronounced at all and some equivalent was used instead. The name of God was considered to be too sacred for everyday use. Its meaning may have been 'he who causes to be', i.e., the

Creator. Certainly this was how the Hebrews thought of God, as Creator of the world and the giver of life. When in 63 B.C. the Roman general Pompey, to the horror of all Jews, strode into the Holy of Holies, the most sacred part of the Temple in Jerusalem and the symbolic dwelling place of YHWH, he was astonished to find no image or statue of the God of the Hebrews. For them God was invisible.

Yet this invisible, undepictable God was for the Hebrews a living presence in their own lives, the guardian of their destiny, controller of the rise and fall of nations and empires. Supreme above all earthly powers, sovereign over all earthly kings and princes, he was also close to all men of humble and contrite spirit.[4] It was this holy, awe-inspiring God who to the never-ending amazement of the Hebrews had chosen them out of all the nations of the earth to be his peculiar people, charged with no less a task than to bring the rest of the world to the knowledge and service of the God who had made himself known to them through their prophets, psalmists and sages. These were the men who had opened their eyes to the meaning and purpose of life, to the mystery and glory of the one true God, to the nature of the obedience he demanded and to the wonder of their own vocation.

Obviously this unique insight into the reality behind the problems and uncertainties of everyday experience did not come to the Hebrews overnight or in a sudden burst of revelation. As we turn the pages of the Old Testament we can trace a deepening understanding of God and a growing apprehension of the many facets of his Being. But it would seem as if the radically new elements which ultimately flowered into such a faith as that expressed in Isaiah 40 or Psalm 103 can be traced back to Moses and the events surrounding the Exodus. To this historical point in time can be dated the beginning of the distinctive Hebrew belief in YHWH as the only true God, a living active power in the affairs of men and nations, in whose service alone can be found the fulfilment of our existence.[5]

There is little to be gained by trying to sift from the mass of legend and later embellishments what exactly happened at the Exodus of the Hebrews from Egypt in the thirteenth century B.C. It is clear that a significant group of the Hebrew people, having enjoyed peace and security for some considerable time as immigrants in Egypt, suddenly found that under a new dynasty they were no longer welcome. Worse than that they were treated as little better than chattels, exploited as unpaid labourers in the building projects of the Pharaoh of the time, and threatened with slow extermination. From this living death they were delivered in some dramatic way about which it is difficult to be precise. The stories of the ten plagues and the crossing of the Red Sea have been coloured by later piety.

Two things are however certain. One is that the Exodus made an indelible impression on all subsequent Hebrew thinking about God. It had not been a mere escape from slavery. It had been a deliverance, a rescue from living death into a new life of freedom and hope. It had been an act of YHWH in which he had shown himself to be Israel's saviour. The second certainty is that without the presence of Moses as their leader to interpret this deliverance as the work of YHWH the sequel to the Exodus would have been vastly different. God had revealed himself to Moses—picturesquely recorded in the symbolic story of the Burning Bush[6]—and summoned him to be the instrument of his purpose. Moses became the channel through which God communicated the truth about himself and his intention to give the Hebrews a unique role among the nations of the ancient world.

However dimly Moses himself may have grasped the implications of this for the future history of the world it was he who laid the foundations of this radically different conception of God as a living active power moulding history and shaping Israel's destiny, and through Israel the destiny of mankind. It was Moses too who interpreted the service of God in terms of moral obedience expressed in the basic code of the Ten Commandments.[7] As was to be expected, and as the subsequent history of Israel shows, this high faith and high morality were beyond the comprehension and attainment of most of the people. But the Old Testament witnesses to the fact that from Moses onwards there were always a few whose hearts and minds were open to receive new understanding and enlightenment from the same God who laid his hand upon them as he had done upon Moses.

It was due to the insights that were given to them, the later prophets of Israel—Amos, Hosea, Jeremiah, Isaiah above all—that the basic picture of God which Moses painted was enriched and enhanced. To one after another some new facet of the nature of God was revealed—his majesty, his holiness, his steadfast love—and something of his purpose that through Israel, his chosen people, this knowledge of what kind of God it is with whom we have to deal should spread to the whole of mankind. To the prophets too was given an increasing awareness of what kind of response such a God expected of men. One of them, Micah, summed it up in this way: What does the Lord require of you but to do justice, and to love kindness, and to walk humbly with your God?[8]

It was this powerful and moving conception of God that the Hebrews handed on to the rest of the world, but in particular to Christianity. For this was the faith that Jesus and his followers inherited, the belief which governed their thoughts. Its implications were comforting and uncomfortable at the same time. As the book of Acts and the letters of the New Testament clearly indicate, when the early Christians focused their worship and obedience on Christ it was not as if he were a rival to or substitute for the God of the Old Testament. He was the God of the Old Testament expressed in human terms, in a way that they could understand.

The whole Bible proclaims, therefore, that the universe in which we live is neither meaningless nor in the hands of Fate, neither at the mercy of some groping Life Force nor directed by some cosmic Mathematician, but governed, controlled and sustained by a Supreme Being whose nature and purpose we can learn above all from the life, teaching, death and resurrection of Jesus of Nazareth.

NOTES

[1] 1 Cor. 8: 5 f. N.E.B.
[2] Deut. 6: 4
[3] Mark 12: 29
[4] Isa. 66: 2
[5] Exod. 6: 3
[6] Exod. 3: 1 ff.
[7] Exod. 20: 1–17
[8] Micah 6: 8 R.S.V.

8

The Significance of Jesus

IF WE SAY 'How odd of God to choose the Jews', we might say in greater bewilderment 'How odd of God to choose Jesus'. It is this paradox which has made it difficult for orthodox Jews, who share with Christians the Old Testament conception of God, to accept that the God of Moses, the God of the later prophets, psalmists and sages of Israel, could have revealed himself finally through this unlikely Galilean carpenter. And yet the faith of the Christian Church is that he did. Remembering that the men and women who were the foundation members of the Church were themselves Jews, how, we may ask, did they, unlike most of their countrymen, come to this conclusion?

One of the problems, if not the major problem, throughout the whole of Hebrew history as recorded in the Old Testament, was to account for the fact that although the Jews were certain that God had singled them out from all the nations and given them a special role, their story had been one of almost unrelieved disaster. Apart from a brief spell of glory in the days of their great king David they had had a never-ending struggle to maintain a foothold in the promised land to which Moses had guided them after their deliverance from Egyptian bondage. One after another more powerful neighbouring states had harassed, pillaged and conquered them. Their capital Jerusalem had been sacked, their sacred Temple laid waste, the cream of the nation carried off to exile in heathen Babylon. Delivered from this once more, as they believed by the mighty hand of YHWH, they had come back to rebuild their holy city and its Temple, only to find themselves doomed to spend the next five centuries as vassals under the heel of one or other of the great empires of the ancient world.

Yet throughout all this time they had an unquenchable hope that this was not God's last word. One day—and sooner rather than later—he would intervene in the affairs of the world to vindicate his people and, more important, to vindicate himself. So strong was their faith in the kind of God they had come to know that they could not think that he would allow his great purpose for the world to be thwarted. It was not the will of God that tyranny, militarism and paganism should flourish for ever but that the nations should be brought into the service of the only true God and live in the right relationship to himself and to one another.

So the Hebrews looked forward to a different kind of world with a different set of values. Instead of hatred and cruelty, inhumanity and violence, there would be peace and righteousness, justice and harmony, not only between men and men but throughout the whole of creation.[1] This splendid vision of a new age and a transformed world called inevitably for a heaven-sent ruler, and equally inevitably their thoughts turned back to David, the nearest approach in their experience to an ideal king. So they looked for someone of the line and type of David, but with qualities that neither David nor any human king could possibly possess. We have only to read Isa. 9: 6–7 and 11: 1–5 to see that their hope of this coming ruler, the Lord's anointed King, the Messiah (our word is simply the Hebrew word 'anointed'), was already leading them to think in terms of someone greater than David, greater than Moses, of someone indeed closely associated with God.

When therefore a small group of Jews, about the year

A.D. 30, began to proclaim in the streets of Jerusalem that the long-awaited Messiah had arrived, and that he was Jesus the carpenter from Nazareth in Galilee, it is not surprising that the Establishment, together with most ordinary Jewish citizens, dismissed them as part of the lunatic fringe. There had already been many charlatans and political adventurers, self-styled Messiahs, whose pretensions had ended in disillusionment for their followers and disaster for themselves.[2] The followers of Jesus, however, claimed that their leader had been different from any of these, and that what had happened to him and to them proved without a shadow of doubt that he was the true Messiah, promised by God through psalmist and prophet. It was left to abler minds than those of the first disciples, notably to St. Paul, to see the full significance of Jesus in the context of God's plan for the renewal of the world, and to give him his proper status not as merely the Messiah of the Jews, but as Lord and Saviour of all mankind.

But what of these first followers of Jesus, these Galileans, mostly simple fishermen? What was it in this small-town joiner that led them to make such extraordinary assertions about him? Undoubtedly it was primarily their belief that his death on a cross had not been the sad fate of yet another victim of Roman oppressors, but that God had miraculously raised him from the tomb to become a living presence in their lives. Yet there was more to it than that. For on reflection they concluded that the Resurrection of Jesus had been the inevitable climax of the life of the man they had known and loved.[3]

The word 'man' is important. The gospels paint a picture not of some shadowy semi-divine figure but of a robust, dynamic man of flesh and blood, hungry, thirsty, tired, depressed and exhilarated in the same way as anyone else. His companions, Peter and the others, were Galileans like himself. They knew his home background, they lived with him night and day throughout the whole time of his mission. He had come into their ken when he was about the age of thirty, having left the obscurity of the small hill-town of Nazareth, to make contact like themselves with the religious revival which was being sponsored at the time by an ascetic preacher reminiscent of an Old Testament prophet, John the Baptist.

Jesus' baptism in the river Jordan at the hands of John seems to have been a decisive experience for him, a summons to action accompanied by a new sense of power. Soon afterwards he launched a mission in his native Galilee, preaching and teaching in synagogues and in the open air. His message was that the new age foretold by the prophets had now begun. God was calling men and women into his service with a new urgency, ready to accept them as they were if they would only commit their lives to him in trust and confidence and with the simplicity of a small child's dependence upon his mother. It was a message that God cared for all his children without discrimination. His will for all was that they should become the sons and daughters of God that they were meant to be. Thus Jesus' emphasis was on right relationships, of men towards God and towards one another, the essence of which was love.

What impressed people about Jesus' teaching was that he spoke with an authority they had never known before. But alongside his teaching, and of equal importance, was his healing of diseased bodies and disturbed minds. The compassion which moved Jesus to heal was, men felt, not only a living illustration of the compassion of God but also a message that God cared for men and women as whole persons, their bodies as well as their souls. It was not his will that sin and sickness should keep them from the enjoyment of the full life which they were meant to have. So Jesus not only restored sight to the blind, sanity to the mentally unbalanced, vigour to the crippled, but also pronounced forgiveness of sin to those who had separated themselves from God by their own folly.

To serious-minded Jews like the few followers who had thrown in their lot with this extraordinary carpenter-

turned-teacher, one of the most striking features of his
teaching was his assumption of the right to criticise the
sacred words of the Law which had been handed down by
the tradition of more than a thousand years as the very
Word of God. What Moses had promulgated as the commands of God for Israel, and through Israel for all mankind, was now radically questioned. Not only did Jesus,
like some of the Old Testament prophets, query the importance of the ceremonial and ritual which centred on
the Temple at Jerusalem, but he also exposed the inadequacy of such a basic code of behaviour as the Ten Commandments.[4] This was more than a protest against the
current debasement of the Temple by avaricious ecclesi-
astics[5] or the pettifogging restrictions on ordinary life by
hair-splitting legal theologians.[6] It was a claim in the
name of God to have the right to set up a new standard
of behaviour and a new interpretation of the true service
of God.

In the light of all this there came the inescapable question: who is this man, this Jesus—an inspired teacher, a
prophet-cum-healer, a religious crank? In the light of his
personal intimacy and his observation of all that had
happened during the Galilean mission, Peter, as spokes-
man of the inner circle of Jesus' followers, who knew him
best, with a flash of insight came to the heart of the truth
when he avowed: You are the Messiah.[7] Jesus had, as the
gospel records show, known this from the moment of his
baptism in the Jordan. He had declared in his public
mission that the new age had come. But because the vast
majority of ordinary people were looking for a Messiah
who would be a military and political challenge to the
Roman oppressors, Jesus had discouraged the use of this
title. He had his own ideas of what kind of Messiah God
wanted him to be.

It would seem that after his baptism at the beginning
of his mission, Jesus had wrestled with this problem, picturesquely described as the Temptation in the Wilder-
ness.[8] He had emerged from this with his mind made up

that the role God demanded of him was that of the
Servant of God depicted by the prophet Isaiah (53: 1 ff.),
who through humiliation, suffering and death would
somehow bring the world to the knowledge of God. No-
one before Jesus had identified the role of the Servant
with the role of the Messiah. But when the Crucifixion
had dealt the death-blow to his disciples' hopes, only to
be followed by the knowledge that God had reversed the
judgment of men by raising Jesus from the dead, it was
this scriptural prophecy of Isaiah that provided them with
the clue to the understanding of the mystery of the Cross.
It had not been a defeat but a triumph. God had vindi-
cated his Servant. Jesus their crucified Master had by the
Resurrection been proved to be the Messiah, or, using the
Greek word, 'the Christ'.

NOTES

[1] Isa. 11: 6 ff.
[2] Acts 5: 34 ff.
[3] Acts 2: 24
[4] Matt. 5: 21 ff.

[5] Mark 11: 15 ff.
[6] Mark 7: 9 ff.
[7] Mark 8: 29 N.E.B.
[8] Matt. 4: 1 ff.

9

The People of God

FROM THE TIME of the Exodus onwards, as we have seen, Israel had thought of itself as different from its neighbours. The Hebrews regarded all nations as being under the sovereign power and purpose of God but they were convinced that they had been singled out in a special way for a special purpose. The Old Testament prophets taught them to see their role not only against the background of recorded history but also against the background of man's existence on the earth. The first eleven chapters of Genesis set the stage for the appearance of Israel as the people of God's choice. There in myth and symbol profound religious truths are conveyed about God and man. It is a graphic picture of our human predicament.

We are shown our world as the creation of a loving God whose will it is that all created things, including man, should live in harmony with one another. Man, however, refuses to accept the authority of God over his life, and through pride and self-will defies his Creator. Yet God, who has made man in his own image, will not write off mankind as an experiment that has failed. He will intervene to rescue man from himself, and so with the twelfth chapter of Genesis begins the story of God's plan for man's salvation which continues through the rest of the Old Testament and finds its fulfilment in the New Testament. Abraham, traditional father of the Hebrew people, is chosen as the foundation member of a community which is to be the instrument of God's purpose to bring the world back to himself. Abraham responds to God's summons and faces an unknown future, trusting only in the promise he has received that his descendants will in some way be the means of winning mankind back to the service of God.[1]

Such was the conviction of their highly improbable destiny, humanly speaking, which was maintained by the foremost of the Hebrew prophets. There was no question in their minds but that this was an unmerited blessing of God. They knew only too well, and said so, that Israel was as a people totally unworthy of this high vocation. Israel as a whole was no better than its neighbours. But God had chosen this unlikely people, despite all its failures, to be the channel of his purpose. Such a vocation was, of course, beyond the comprehension of most. To be God's chosen people meant for the majority of the Hebrews to be more powerful, more successful, more impressive than their neighbours. Only Isaiah, among the prophets, and the unknown author of the book of Jonah, saw the vocation of their people as one which involved the enlightenment of the despised heathen—and for Isaiah, this would also involve suffering, humiliation and death.[2]

The bond which linked God with his people was the Covenant, established at Sinai after the Exodus, by which YHWH pledged himself to Israel and Israel pledged itself to YHWH, accepting the Ten Commandments as its basic rule of life.[3] Throughout the ups and downs of Israel's subsequent history, prophet after prophet condemned the nation for its failure to live in accordance with these basic obligations, which were later expanded into the corpus of teaching known as the Torah or Law, and are contained in the first five books of the Old Testament. Yet there was always a faithful minority which maintained the austere standards of belief and practice stemming from these early days. Men of the calibre of

Samuel, Nathan, Elijah and Micaiah reminded kings and commoners alike of Israel's unique vocation, before the great spokesmen of YHWH, Amos, Hosea, Isaiah, Jeremiah, Ezekiel and the rest of the prophets, spelt out for the men of their day what was demanded of a people of God. When the very existence of the nation was threatened Isaiah held out the hope that whatever happened there would be a faithful Remnant[4] which would maintain Israel's historic role, and Jeremiah looked for a day when God would make a new Covenant with his people, not written on tablets of stone like the Ten Commandments but written on men's hearts.[5]

It is clear from the New Testament (the word Testament itself means Covenant) that Jesus and his disciples regarded themselves as the Remnant of Israel embodying the new Covenant. Jesus himself did not use the word 'remnant', although St. Paul does,[6] but in his choice of twelve disciples he was obviously creating a new Israel which would be called on to fulfil the mission which the twelve tribes of old Israel had failed to accomplish. He was founding a reformed people of God, built on the highest expression of the faith and practice of the Old Testament but purified of its dead wood and nationalist limitations. When at the Last Supper he broke the bread and shared the wine with his followers, he described his impending death as the new Covenant, making possible the new relationship with God of which Jeremiah had spoken.

It was with this conviction that they were the historical inheritors of the role of the people of God, charged with the same task of bringing the world to the knowledge and service of God, that the first Christians after Pentecost set out from Jerusalem to 'make disciples of all nations',[7] beginning with their own countrymen. It was a daunting enterprise, calling for more than ordinary human courage and resolution. To their fellow Jews they appeared in the earliest days of their mission to be harmless cranks. They complied with the traditions and obligations of

Jewish Law, and if on top of this they had the strange delusion that their former leader Jesus of Nazareth was indeed the long-awaited Messiah, they were to be tolerated—and perhaps pitied—rather than opposed.

For the disciples of Jesus, however, their position was quite different. They were not sustained by nostalgic recollections of a martyred prophet but by the knowledge that their Master, who had been crucified and laid in a tomb, had been raised by God from the dead, had appeared to them and spoken to them, and who had since that unforgettable moment on the first Whitsunday empowered them by his Spirit to continue his work of teaching and healing. What they were doing, therefore, was not dependent on their own poor efforts but on the supernatural power of God. It is impossible to account for the transformation of a handful of simple Galilean fishermen into the spearhead of a world-wide missionary movement other than by the recognition that something unique had happened in the history and experience of mankind.

It was this sense of transformation that led the first Christians to ask themselves: then who can this Jesus of Nazareth have been? Already their Jewish upbringing had taught them to think of the Messiah as someone whom no normal category could contain. But as they looked back on their experiences with this enigmatic prophet from Nazareth, and as they remembered his extraordinary power of conveying a sense of the presence of God, as they remembered his words and actions, they moved inescapably to draw more startling conclusions. What had been most striking about Jesus had been his attitude to God. He had taught his followers to approach God as a heavenly Father who cared for them as his children in a way that no earthly father could attain to. But Jesus himself had spoken of his own relationship to God in a unique way. He might choose to call himself Son of Man, his disciples might recognise him as the long-awaited Messiah who had taken upon himself the role of the Servant, but underneath any such titles was the basic sense of his oneness with God, evidenced by all that he said and did.

As we turn the pages of the Fourth Gospel, where more than anywhere else in the New Testament we find Jesus speaking of his relationship to God as that of Father and Son, we cannot always be sure whether the words are the exact words of Jesus or the words of a beloved disciple after a lifetime's reflection on what Jesus had come to mean for him. But the portrait of Jesus given in the Fourth Gospel complements the picture of him given by the other three gospels and does not contradict it. It makes explicit what is implicit—and occasionally also explicit[8]—in Mark, Matthew and Luke. It was the cumulative effect of reflection on the past and experience in the present that led the early Christians to acknowledge Jesus as their Saviour and their Lord. They prayed to him and worshipped him, not identifying him fully with God—their Jewish monotheism prevented this—but proclaiming him as God's Son who had come among men and shared their life, and who was now exalted to his proper place at the right hand of God.[9] In such pictorial language, Christians from the beginning expressed their conviction of the unique status of Christ, which in time came to be embodied in the creeds of the Church.

The word 'Church' itself (ekklesia), which the early Christians used to describe the community to which they belonged, was no accidental choice. It was the word which had been used in the Greek version of the Old Testament to describe Israel as the chosen people of God. In adopting it for themselves the first Christians emphasised their sense of continuity with old Israel. Their role in the world within God's plan to save mankind from the consequences of his own folly was to be that of the Israel of God,[10] the people of his choice charged with the responsibility of taking the Good News of his love to all the nations.

When St. Paul describes the Church as the Body of

Christ, as he does so frequently, he pinpoints the difference between the Church and any other society or organisation. It is a unique community, bound together in allegiance to Christ as its Head, to carry on Christ's work in the world in the power of his Spirit. In Old Testament times it was hard for the Hebrews most of the time to see their role as the people of God in anything but racially exclusive terms. The nations of the world must turn to the Jews, and become Jews, in order to reach the right relationship with God and find fulfilment of life.

As we can see from the New Testament the new people of God, the Church, the Body of Christ, under the prompting—and prodding—of the Spirit was led to see its role quite otherwise. It was to be supranational not national, inclusive not exclusive, barrier-breaking not barrier-creating. Its message was that God accepts men as they are and invites them to a life of service within the fellowship of his people—Jews and Gentiles, slaves and freemen, male and female, rich and poor, young and old. The keynote was reconciliation of man to God and men with each other, of renewal of the whole fabric of society, political, social and economic, by the Spirit of Christ working through those who had committed their lives to him.

NOTES

[1] Gen. 12: 1 ff; 15: 6; Gal. 3: 6
[2] Isa. 53
[3] Exod. 24: 3 ff; 20: 1 ff.
[4] Isa. 10: 20 f.
[5] Jer. 31: 31 ff.
[6] Rom. 9: 27 ff.
[7] Matt. 28: 19 R.S.V.
[8] e.g. Matt. 11: 27; Luke 10: 22
[9] Phil. 2: 5 ff.
[10] Gal. 6: 16

10

Belief in Man

IT IS A STRIKING fact that in a book which is so God-centred as the Bible there is at the same time a tremendous emphasis on the importance of man. There is, of course, no suggestion that he is self-sufficient. He owes his existence to God like the rest of creation. In the picturesque imagery of Genesis 'the Lord God formed man of dust from the ground'.[1] We are, as St. Paul says, 'of the earth, earthy',[2] part of the animal kingdom, sustained like the beasts by the fruits of the soil on which we tread, and like them returning to it when we die. Ecclesiastes spells out the message for us with his wonted realism: 'For the fate of the sons of men and the fate of beasts is the same; as one dies, so dies the other. They all have the same breath, and man has no advantage over the beasts ... All go to one place; all are from the dust, and all turn to dust again.'[3]

Yet this is far from being all that the Bible has to say about us. If it were we should have little to quarrel about with the Stalins and the Hitlers who regard human lives as having no more significance than weeds or flies, to be destroyed like pests and with as little compunction. But the Bible makes it plain that this is a crime against the Creator, for, as we are told,[4] 'God created man in his own image, in the image of God he created him; male and female he created them.' However we interpret the meaning of 'image', there is quite clearly something about human beings which differentiates them from the rest of the created world to which they belong.

The psalmist thinks of this difference in terms of man's power over nature, and his words are strikingly confirmed in our own day more than ever before. 'Thou hast made him little less than God, and dost crown him with glory and honour. Thou hast given him dominion over the works of thy hands; thou hast put all things under his feet...'[5] When we look at the marvels of modern technology and electronics or watch on television men walking on the moon, and speculate on greater triumphs of science still to come, the psalmist would seem to have possessed uncanny insight into the future. Little wonder that some would echo Swinburne's outburst: 'Glory to man in the highest, for man is the master of things', and would go on to ask: is there any need for a God at all?

But according to the Bible the difference between man and the rest of creation is not simply that he has the power and skill to harness natural resources and use them for the enrichment of his life. This is indeed an important aspect of his activities but it does not touch his essential nature. When we are told that we are made in the 'image' of God after his 'likeness',[6] it means more than a delegated authority to exercise control over some aspects of nature similar to that which God exercises over the whole universe. It rather implies that there is a point of contact between God and man which is not shared by anything else in the world. There is an affinity between God and man which makes it possible for them to enter into a relationship with one another, to speak to one another. St. Augustine pinpointed this truth and reached the essence of what the Bible says about man when he said: 'Thou hast made us for thyself, and the heart of man is restless until it finds its rest in thee.'

The message of the Bible is that our life comes from God and finds meaning and purpose only when we acknowledge our dependence on him and recognise his authority over us. But it is equally the message of the

Bible that this is precisely what mankind as a whole has never been prepared to do. The tragedy of our human situation is marvellously depicted in the form of symbolic stories in the early chapters of Genesis. Adam and Eve represent, of course, men and women as they have always been. Given freedom to run their lives as they choose, subject to the sovereign authority of God, they flout that authority and seek to put themselves in God's place—to set their own standards, to decide for themselves what is good and what is evil.[7] They end up by destroying the right relationship with God and with one another. They put a barrier between themselves and God.

Relentlessly the Bible exposes our predicament. Disobedience in the father (Adam) leads to hate and murder in the son (Cain)[8] and the power of evil becomes a corruption of the whole cosmos.[9] With the onward march of civilisation man's pride and selfishness reach ever greater heights and bring more widespread disaster (the Tower of Babel).[10] Little wonder that the Bible's sober verdict on us is that the wickedness of man is great in the earth and that every imagination of the thoughts of his heart is only evil continually, or that it pictures God as regretting that he had brought mankind into being.[11] God's purpose that all created things should live in harmony with each other and with their Creator has been thwarted. In particular, men and women who were meant to live as sons and daughters under a heavenly Father have replaced love to God with love of self. Thus the Bible traces the confusion and bitterness in our disordered society, the violence, greed and cruelty of man towards his neighbour, to the basic problem of man's selfishness. It is due to this radical twist in man's nature, this tendency to make himself the centre of the universe instead of God, that man finds himself hell-bent on his own destruction.

The short biblical word for all this is sin. The Greek word for it means literally 'missing the mark', and this is essentially what sin is. St. Paul calls it falling short of the glory of God,[12] separating ourselves from God, putting a gulf between ourselves and him. This is man's perennial plight for, again in St. Paul's words which all of us know to be true: 'I do not understand my own actions. For I do not do what I want, but I do the very thing I hate ... I do not do the good I want, but the evil I do not want is what I do.'[13] Sin and the subsequent sense of guilt that haunts us when we have done things that our conscience tells us are wrong are regarded by many today as old-fashioned ideas that are best forgotten. But any psychiatrist will tell us, whatever terms he uses to describe them, that they are as real in the twentieth century as in biblical times, and that a whole variety of emotional upsets and nervous disorders can be traced to these very things.

St. Paul has often been accused of overplaying his hand and of having been obsessed with the problem of man's sinfulness. But Jesus was no less emphatic,[14] nor indeed were the psalmists and the prophets of the Old Testament.[15] We shall never understand what the Bible has to say about man until we recognise the fact that all men are sinners in need of forgiveness, not least ourselves. It has always been the most saintly men and women who have been most conscious of their failure. If we come to terms with the biblical insight that all of us are by nature selfish, acquisitive and calculating, and that man's primary motive is self-interest, we shall be saved from shallow optimism about the future of our society. We shall not be surprised that every good enterprise and every venture into social reform is abused and exploited. The more complex our civilisation becomes the more opportunities it affords for unscrupulous manipulators. The Christian doctrine of Original Sin, which is simply the recognition that all men always are and always have been selfish, is basic to our proper understanding of man.

But if the Bible forbids us to be blindly optimistic about man's power sooner or later to set the world to rights, equally it discourages us from being depressingly pessimistic. For the dismal picture of man suggested by the colourful stories at the beginning of Genesis, which add up to a cosmic version of Hogarth's *Rake's Progress*, is a picture of man without the Gospel, of man left to himself. And this is precisely what the Bible says man never has been. For the whole Bible is the story of what God has done and is still doing to save man from himself, to rescue him from his plight, to do for him what he cannot do for himself. Mankind for all its crimes and follies is not left, like Cain, to be 'a fugitive and a wanderer on the earth',[16] for man, even the murderous Cain, is made in the image of God. Already, in the biblical imagery, God has not written off the disobedient Adam and Eve; he has made for them 'garments of skins, and clothed them',[17] symbolic of his providential care. So also he puts his mark of protection even on murderous Cain. So also he recognises that humanity is worth saving for the sake of one good pagan, Noah,[18] neither a Jew nor a Christian, who lived by the light of conscience, the rudimentary knowledge of God which has been given to all men, since all men are made in the image of God.

The Bible is undisguisedly and inescapably a message of the supernatural power of God to influence men's lives and to change them from what they are to what they ought to be. When St. Paul speaks of the Gentiles as having the law of God 'written on their hearts' he is affirming that to men of all religions—and in our own day this would mean adherents of all the great world religions—God has given some knowledge of himself and of the meaning and purpose of life. But through Israel and especially through the one true Israelite who was wholly obedient to God, Jesus of Nazareth, God has given a revelation of what man can become, which is what man was meant to be, and has also given him the power to fulfil that destiny. Man who is made in the image of God, which by his sinfulness he has so grotesquely distorted that he has become a caricature of his real self, can by the grace of God, and only by the grace of God, be changed into the child of God which is his true role.

As we trace through the Old Testament the majestic drama of the acts of God to save man from himself, we see God calling men into his service, as he did with Abraham, Moses and the great prophets of Israel. We are told how splendidly they responded, and how through them the psalmists and sages of Israel were brought face to face with God and how they in their turn have awakened countless more in their day and ever since, to acknowledge the presence and help of God in their lives. In the New Testament we read how ordinary men and women in Galilee and Judaea found their lives transformed by their encounter with Jesus, and how after his Resurrection countless equally ordinary men and women, named and unnamed, from every nation came to know God through the Spirit of the risen Christ. From Pentecost onwards up to the present day millions have found through the fellowship of the Church in all its branches that life has taken on a new meaning and has a new purpose. Through Christ they have come to know the love of God and the power of his forgiveness. With all their human limitations they have begun to be the sons and daughters of God that they will more fully become hereafter.

NOTES

[1] Gen. 2: 7
[2] 1 Cor. 15: 47
[3] Eccles. 3: 19 f. R.S.V.
[4] Gen. 1: 27 R.S.V.
[5] Ps. 8: 5 R.S.V.
[6] Gen. 1: 26
[7] Gen. 3: 1 ff.
[8] Gen. 4: 1 ff.
[9] Gen. 6: 1 ff.

[10] Gen. 11: 1 ff.
[11] Gen. 6: 5 ff.
[12] Rom. 3: 23
[13] Rom. 7: 15 ff. R.S.V.
[14] John 8: 7
[15] Ps. 51: 1 ff; Isa. 6: 5
[16] Gen. 4: 12 R.S.V.
[17] Gen. 3: 21 R.S.V.
[18] Gen. 6: 8 f.

What This Means for Us Today

II

Guidelines for Action

HALFWAY THROUGH HIS letter to the Ephesians St. Paul dramatically changes key. In the first half of the letter he has swept the strings and lifted our hearts until we seem to stand in the very forecourt of heaven as he unfolds the glory and the mystery of God's plan for man's salvation through Christ. Then, magnificently, he brings us down to earth and tells us what all this means in terms of practical day-to-day living. How does the message of the Gospel affect us in our homes, in our jobs, as members of our society? Significantly he begins the second half of his letter with the word 'therefore',[1] and goes on to show the implications of Christian faith for Christian action. Because we so believe, he is saying, this is how we must live.

Similarly we may now ask ourselves what does the message of the Bible as a whole mean for us today? How does what the Bible tells us about God and man, about Jesus and his Church, affect us in the unspectacular roles in the community which most of us have to play? We are neither statesmen with the power to mould the destiny of nations, nor tycoons of industry and commerce with the power to affect for good or ill the livelihood of thousands or tens of thousands. We are just ordinary people, so ordinary that we may be tempted to ask: do we matter to God or to anyone else? This is no new question. Among others Isaiah was faced with it. The dejected exiles in

Babylon complained that God must have forgotten them. Isaiah's answer was that God's care for all his children is never ceasing, and that 'those who look to the Lord will win new strength'.[2] St. Paul answers the second half of our question in his letter to the Ephesians when he tells them that each of us has been given some gift to be used in God's service, and that whoever we are we each have a part to play in 'the building up of the body of Christ',[3] which simply means the service of mankind. Fine words indeed, but what do they mean in practice?

The Gospel as Christ declared it has been described as a message of whole salvation and not just soul salvation. Christ healed men's bodies as well as their minds and was concerned that the poor should not go hungry.[4] And as St. Theresa has said, those who have committed their lives to him are his hands and feet to do his bidding in the world and he has no others. The needs of the world's hungry millions must be on all our consciences and we are bound to give of our means as we can to help them. This is a basic humanitarian service which the Christian shares with men and women of all religions or of none. But the Christian helps because he believes that the hungry millions are all his brothers and sisters for whom Christ died. When Jesus told the story of the Good Samaritan[5] he was answering the question: who is my neighbour? which a lawyer had put to him when he had confirmed that love towards God and one's neighbour is the twin obligation on all who seek to inherit eternal life. In the story it is made plain that in Jesus' view our neighbour is simply anyone who needs our help.

But as has sometimes been pointed out the Good Samaritan had a relatively easy assignment. He found a wounded man by the roadside. He had the equipment handy to render first-aid, and enough money in his pocket to pay for the victim's maintenance in a neighbouring hospice. Things do not generally work out so simply in our complex modern society. We know, for example, that housing conditions in parts of our great cities are a scandal and an affront to a relatively affluent nation. We know too that there is discrimination in this country against coloured immigrants who have legally every right to live here as members of the British Commonwealth which we have created. Likewise we know that in this youth-obsessed period of our history the plight of the lonely and undernourished old person is a reproach to all of us. The splendid voluntary work of housing associations, societies for the protection of the rights of coloured citizens, and organisations which are active on behalf of old people's welfare, such as the W.R.V.S. with its Meals-on-Wheels service, mitigates the hardship but emphasises the magnitude of the problem. Whether we like it or not, the solution of these and similar blots on our society rests ultimately in the field of politics.

This is for many Christian people an unpleasant and disappointing conclusion. It would be so much easier if the issues were presented in black and white, as they were to the Good Samaritan. But they are not. And Christians must come to recognise that our choices are not between black and white but between various shades of grey. There are no easy answers. Why, moreover, we may ask, does the Bible not give us clear and unmistakable guidance on the great international issues that confront us in the seventies? Most of us would probably feel that the policy and practice of apartheid is one of the major blots on the record of the white man in Africa. We coveted the Africans' land and its resources, and took them guns, cash and Bibles. Now as they tell us bitterly, they have our Bible and we have their land. But how are we to help our black fellow-Christians who suffer under South Africa's unjust penal laws against them? By encouraging them to revolt, or by joining demonstrations against all-white sports teams visiting this country? On a matter like this the Bible gives us no clear guidance. Nor does it tell us how to deal effectively with the recurrent danger of outbreaks of anti-semitism, or which side to support in the Arab–Israeli conflict or, nearer home, how to solve the Ulster problem, which is at least partly religious.

The pages of the Old Testament are stained with the bloodshed of endless battles. Yet amidst the carnage some looked forward to the day when 'nation shall not lift up sword against nation, neither shall they learn war any more'.[6] In the light of the Gospel, to say nothing of natural revulsion from the horrible refinements of modern weapons—napalm and the like—war must be abhorrent to every Christian conscience. But if war becomes national policy—as in the case of the United States in Vietnam—what is the Christian duty of the individual? To be a pacifist, to be a reluctant combatant, to help the war effort in some non-military capacity? Again the Bible gives us no clear answer. Nor can the Bible be cited in defence of capitalist materialism as opposed to communist materialism, any more than it can tell us whether to vote Conservative, Labour or Liberal.

On the vexed social issues of our day it is no accident that among the avowed Christian members of Parliament, opposing views can be taken on questions of the rights and wrongs of contraception and abortion, the use of 'soft' drugs, the legalisation of homosexual practices between consenting adults, sex education in schools, nudity on stage and screen, and the various other problems of what has come to be known as our 'permissive society'. On the industrial front is it the duty of a Christian trade unionist to come out on strike in support of a fellow-worker who, as he believes, has been wrongfully dismissed by the management, although thereby he may be imperilling production and perhaps the future of his firm? We could go on interminably citing cases where the Christian as a citizen, as an employer or an employee, as a father or mother of a family, or simply as a convinced member of Christ's Church, must come to some decision one way or the other. And, it must be said again, the Bible gives us no clear answers. Why is this?

The Bible does indeed give us an answer, but it is not

an easy one. For, as we have seen, the richness and the glory of our humanity is that God has left us free to make our own choices. We are not puppets, but men and women who have to choose from day to day in the light of the alternatives that confront us, what we shall do and what course of action we shall commend, taking full responsibility for the consequences. If our choices are wrong and if disaster overtakes us or our society, let us not blame God. This is the penalty and the glory of our freedom. But who would wish it otherwise? This is surely what makes life exhilarating. No one wants to be a computerised automaton. From the story of Adam and Eve onwards the Bible is a tale of choices, for what is right against what is wrong, for the light against the darkness, for God against the power of evil. Yet in the daily choices that we, like the people of the Bible, have to make, the issues are seldom if ever presented in such starkly simple terms. For most of the time we have to compromise between the ideal and the practicable. In an imperfect world usually the best we can do is to choose the lesser of two evils. We have to make our decisions on the great social and political issues as well as on the personal issues that confront us daily, by weighing up the pros and cons and acting in accordance with what we believe is most in harmony with the will and purpose of God. The difficulty is of course that often in a given situation it is by no means certain what the will and purpose of God may be.

But the Bible by no means leaves us without guidance. We are given a series of signposts pointing in the general direction which we must follow. Our path ahead is not plotted out for us. We have to pick our own steps, and undoubtedly some of these steps will be false ones. We may be able to retrace them or we may sometimes find ourselves plunging deeper into the mire. But we cannot finally lose our way as individuals or as a society if we follow the signposts which God has given us in the Old and New Testaments. There is a great mass of detailed

instructions for day-to-day living contained in the first
five books of the Old Testament, the Law by which the
common life of the Hebrews was controlled. As they believed, this was the will of God for his people. In many of
the psalms we see how the study of the Law could be an
aid to devotion, an inspiration and a gateway into the
presence of God.[7]

But by the time of Jesus, in the hands of the Pharisees,
and the ecclesiastical lawyers, the Law had become a
stranglehold. Ordinary men and women found its observ-
ance a joyless burden. Jesus sought to sweep aside the
deadwood and come to the heart of the matter. There
were said to be six hundred and thirteen commandments
in Old Testament Law. Jesus singled out two of these[8]
and made them the supreme rule of life for his followers:
'You shall love the Lord your God with all your heart,
and with all your soul, and with all your mind, and with
all your strength', and 'you shall love your neighbour as
yourself'.[9] These are not so much two commandments as
a twin commandment. For we cannot love God without
loving our neighbour, and in loving our neighbour we
are expressing our love to God. In the Sermon on the
Mount Jesus summarises Christian behaviour in the
Golden Rule—'Whatever you wish that men would do to
you, do so to them; for this is the Law and the Prophets.'[10]

There are indeed signposts for our guidance in Old
Testament Law, notably the Ten Commandments,[11]
which still provide us with valuable pointers to the principles on which Christian life should be based. Jesus does
not regard them as outmoded but shows what they mean
for us at their deepest level.[12] Similarly, the Old Testament Prophets have given us guidelines for action, perhaps best summarised in the words of one of them
already quoted: 'What does the Lord require of you but
to do justice, and to love kindness, and to walk humbly
with your God?'[13] Again the words of Jesus distil for us
the message of the prophets. His teaching has been de-

scribed as a compass to give us direction, rather than an ordnance map to control our every step. This may be said to be true of the whole message of the Bible as it affects the choices and decisions that we have to make every day of our lives, in personal relationships and in our judgments on social and political issues in our own country or farther afield.

The Bible as a whole makes it plain that we can satisfactorily run our own lives and the life of the community, or for that matter of the world, only if we recognise that we are all responsible to God and not only to ourselves. It tells us that *all* men and women are made in the image of God and that therefore they are our 'neighbours', to be treated with the same concern and respect as we should want to be treated with ourselves. The Australian aboriginal, the African Bantu, the American Red Indian and other victims of the white man's expansionist policies are as much children of the God who gave us all life as we are. But so are the aged and the lonely, the maladjusted and the misfits, the juvenile delinquents, the drop-outs, the alcoholics and the hippies. The short answer as to how to deal with such as these—which was Hitler's answer—cannot be *our* answer if we take the Bible seriously. In all cases there is need for understanding, compassion, tolerance and patience—qualities with which few of us are naturally endowed. When Jesus tells us to love our neighbour as ourselves is he then asking us to do the impossible?

NOTES

[1] Eph. 4: 1
[2] Isa. 40: 31 N.E.B.
[3] Eph. 4: 7 ff. N.E.B.
[4] Mark 10: 21
[5] Luke 10: 29 ff.
[6] Isa. 2: 4
[7] Ps. 1: 1 f.
[8] Deut. 6: 4; Lev. 19: 18
[9] Mark 12: 28 ff. R.S.V.
[10] Matt. 7: 12 R.S.V.
[11] Exod. 20: 1 ff.
[12] Matt. 5: 17 ff.
[13] Micah 6: 8 R.S.V.

12

Sources of Power

IN A SENSE THE reply to the question at the end of the last
chapter must be Yes. Equally impossible to fulfil is Jesus'
demand that we should love God with all our heart, soul,
mind and strength. No doubt some of the saints in Christian history have come close to achieving the impossible.
But as we look round our friends and acquaintances, and
above all when we look at ourselves, we see no saints but
imperfect and very ordinary men and women who with
the best will in the world are baffled by many of the
problems of daily living and quite unable to put their
love of God or their neighbour before their love of themselves. From time to time we read in the press of some act
of heroism where a man gives his own life to save the life
of another, and we are humbled and moved, as we are
also by the example of someone in our own circle of
friends whose selfless devotion to a spastic child, a
crippled husband, a bed-ridden parent or an ailing wife
makes us feel that this is the stuff that saints are made of.
But for most of us, most of the time, self-interest comes
first.

Jesus accepts this as the natural human condition. He
assumes that we love ourselves best and urges us to try to
love our neighbour just as much. He brackets both with
love towards God. And no-one but Jesus himself has ever
fully achieved this, which is why he is unique. But if the
coming of Christ on to the stage of human history had

simply meant that we have been given an example of how life should be lived it would be an inspiring experience but also a frustrating one. And it is the message of the New Testament that the Good News is not merely that Christ has shown us the way but that he has given us the power to follow it as well. And this is the reason for the existence of the Church and the only vindication of its chequered history.

The Church in all its branches is going through a period of reappraisal and renewal. To many this appears to be much more a period of decline leading to extinction. Certainly statistics seem to point in this direction and the closing down of redundant buildings, dwindling participation by young people in the various organisations of the Church and the increasingly middle-aged or elderly appearance of most congregations contrast unfavourably with the heyday of Victorian and Edwardian churchmanship. Many have lost interest and withdrawn their support because they find the form of worship irrelevant or boring, others because they feel that the 'Church', by which they mean its spokesmen, does not provide instant answers to the complex problems that confront the modern world. Others again understand only too well what the Church stands for and do not want to be committed.

This has all happened before. Conventional Victorian piety like the Empire which encouraged it was a passing phase. It is a gain that it is no longer the hall-mark of respectability to be a regular church-attender. The Church has always been truest to itself and to its Founder when it has been a minority movement, as critical of itself as of the society it seeks to serve. We must not think of the mission of the People of God as having been exhausted in the successes and failures of the last two thousand years of Church history, any more than it was in the two thousand years of Israel's history before that. For all we know its mission may extend millions of years ahead of us now, in circumstances that are as yet unimaginable

and certainly unpredictable. Whether the Church in anything like its present form will last for another thousand
years it is impossible to say and it is idle to speculate. The
existence of the People of God does not depend on buildings, an organised ministry or a formal liturgy. But it
does involve people meeting together. Since they must
meet somewhere this implies buildings of some kind, and
since everyone cannot be allowed to speak at once, this
also suggests some kind of order. Apart from such vague
requirements we may leave the future structure of the
Church an open question.

Jesus said: 'Where two or three are gathered together
in my name, there am I in the midst of them'.[1] He also
said that the power of evil would never prevail against
the Church which he founded on Peter, the Rock.[2] It is
basically because these promises have been found to be
true that small groups of people who believe that for
them Christ is the Way, the Truth and the Life, still
come together in an age of scepticism and confusion. It
may be that they are attending Mass, or participating in
the Eucharist, or joining in some simpler form of worship. But whatever the form of service may be they find
that in the fellowship of the Church they are brought
into touch with God and get inspiration and help for the
day-to-day business of life.

Many would find it difficult to put into words precisely
why they continue to go to Church in a non-churchgoing
age. Some are following the habit of a lifetime, others
maintain that they go for the sake of their husbands or
wives or children. Some would claim that the services of
the Church bring them closer to what lies behind the
mystery of our existence, others again feel that what they
hear in Church reminds them of the moral principles on
which their own daily conduct should be based. There
are many gateways into the presence of God and many
channels through which he communicates with those who
would serve him. But in the last resort people go to
Church because they find that it helps them to be the

kind of people they would like to be and ought to be and try to be.

The old-fashioned name for the help that the Church gives is 'the means of grace'. This is simply saying that in the services of the Church—through the sacraments, the scriptures, preaching, praise and prayer—power from God comes into our lives provided our hearts and minds are open to him. Some people can trace a change in their lives to some specific moment when God has spoken to them and challenged them in the words of some inspired preacher, or in some arresting passage of scripture, or in some mystical experience on a sacramental occasion. For most who still value the help that the Church can give it is, however, more likely to be a slow and subconscious influence upon us which we recognise as gradually changing our attitude to ourselves and to our neighbours, in our homes, in our jobs and in the society in which we live.

In his great letter to the Galatians[3] St. Paul contrasts the kind of behaviour that comes naturally to us—lust, envy, bad temper, jealousy and selfish ambition—with the kind of behaviour that becomes possible when we let ourselves be influenced by God's Spirit—love, patience, kindness, fidelity and self-control. These are attributes which we cannot acquire by ourselves. Only the supernatural power of God working upon and within us can achieve them for us. Paul sees life as a constant battle where our natural tendencies are at war with what we know to be the kind of behaviour that God requires as he has shown us in Christ. And we are assured that we do not fight this battle alone but that God's Spirit within us is fighting for us. Every time we respond to the voice of conscience it is a victory for the Spirit.

It goes without saying that anyone who claims to be a Christian should be recognisable as someone who can be trusted, who is honest in money matters, keeps his promises, does a fair day's work for a fair day's wage, cares for his family, is kind to animals and lends a helping

hand as and when he can. There are wider issues in
society, however, where Christians may rightly differ in
their attitudes and behaviour. Thus while all Christians
must hate war it is possible to find in the same congregation or Christian group some who believe that this in-
volves commitment to pacifism and others who believe
that the cause of peace is best served by membership of
the armed forces.

All Christians must deplore drunkenness as an affront
to the image of God in which we are made, but again
only some will see in this an obligation to practise total
abstinence. While all Christians will disapprove of gam-
bling when it becomes an obsession, many will regard an
occasional 'flutter' as harmless. Sexual promiscuity and
pornography must be abhorrent to all Christians as
destructive of marriage and family life and a possible corruption of impressionable children. Fidelity within marriage and chastity before marriage are properly regarded
as the Christian norm, yet there are circumstances where
marriage for one reason or another is not possible when a
genuine love relationship without benefit of clergy may
be regarded as marriage in the sight of God.

In the Sermon on the Mount[4] Jesus did not prescribe
a code of behaviour which must be literally or slavishly
followed. To turn the other cheek[5] could on occasion be
a highly provocative act; to assist a murderer on his way[6]
would be no part of Christian conduct and to disburse
charity indiscriminately[7] could have disastrous consequences. To love our enemies,[8] i.e., private individuals
who have a grudge against us, does not mean that we are
expected to like them but that we should try to see their
point of view. Liking or disliking our enemies—or for
that matter our neighbours—has little to do with loving
them. Love in the Christian sense is not based on instinc-
tive and usually irrational reactions but on willingness
to try to understand and sympathise with others' needs
and to help where and when we can.

It is here that prayer comes to our aid. Public prayer

has been described as an unnatural act and many feel that, as Jesus said, prayer is best made privately.[9] Yet Jesus himself attended the synagogue where the thoughts of the congregation were directed towards God by a spoken liturgy and this is still true in the Church, whether the forms used are ancient or modern. But of course when Christians speak of the value of prayer they generally mean the regular practice of personal conversation with God. It would be tiresome to list here the variety of ways in which the use of prayer has been misunderstood. It may be said, however, that prayer is not an attempt to wrest favours from God to benefit ourselves, or to make God change his mind, but primarily an offering of ourselves to God to be used for his purposes.

We would do well in our private prayers to be guided by the traditional pattern of the public prayers of the Church. We shall want to thank God daily for all his goodness to us, for life itself and a measure of health, for the beauty of the created world, for home and family and friends. We shall want to acknowledge our daily failure to live as God would have us live and to ask for his forgiveness. We shall pray for his blessing on all those whom we know to be working in the spirit of Christ in our own land or overseas, on those whom we know to be suffering in body or to be troubled in mind, on all those who are near and dear to us. If we are guided by the supreme pattern of all prayer,[10] as Jesus has taught us, our prayer for ourselves will be that God will use us to bring our common life on earth a little closer to life as it is lived in heaven, that he will help us to overcome the temptations that beset us and the power of evil that surrounds us. Many find that frequent momentary recollections of God, 'arrow-prayers', come most easily to them.

It is impossible to overestimate the power of prayer. It was in his constant communion with his Father that Jesus found strength to help and heal, guidance to speak and courage to act. He became the Man for Others because he was basically the Man for God. It may well be that the current cults of pop music, occultism, astrology and Eastern mysticism among fringe elements in the younger generation including, significantly, what is being called 'The Jesus Revolution' in the United States, is not simply a revolt against conventional religion or a protest against civilisation, but a questing of the human spirit for something beyond the material benefits which are the present obsession of the Western world. In a time of disillusionment with all accepted institutions such as parliamentary government and organised religion, and with all spurious panaceas such as are offered by scientific progress and universal education, we may be coming slowly and tortuously—which is the way human affairs work—to a recovery of more wholesome and stable foundations on which to build our future. In this dissatisfaction with the present and longing for something better, can we look to the Bible for help?

NOTES

[1] Matt. 18: 20
[2] Matt. 16: 18
[3] Gal. 5: 13 ff.
[4] Matt. 5–7
[5] Matt. 5: 39
[6] Matt. 5: 41
[7] Matt. 5: 42
[8] Matt. 5: 44
[9] Matt. 6: 6
[10] Matt. 6: 9 ff.

13

How the Bible Helps

THE ARGUMENT OF this book is that in a changing world and in face of an uncertain future the Bible provides us with an anchor to reality and with guidance for living. God's purpose for us, in Jesus' words, is that we should have life in all its fullness.[1] The Church exists to be the channel through which the supernatural power of God comes into men's lives and through them infiltrates into society, as men and women who acknowledge Christ as Lord seek to live by the light of the Gospel in their homes and in their jobs, and try in their own sphere of influence, however small, to bring our common life more into harmony with the mind and example of Jesus.

But, as we have seen, the organised Church in all its branches is for a variety of reasons making less and less impact upon the community at large and attracting fewer and fewer people to its services. Is it too much to hope that some who now feel that the Church has little to say to them might find that in reading and thinking about what the Bible proclaims they are not only given new understanding of what life is about but also new insight into the value and purpose of the Church itself? Clearly private Bible reading is no substitute for full participation in Christian fellowship yet time and again when organised Christianity has failed to speak to men's needs it has been the study of the Bible which has paved the way for a massive revitalising of the Church and, through the Church, of society as a whole.

It was the inspiration that came from reading the scriptures in the monasteries that sent the friars out into the Europe of the Dark Ages with a message that brought enlightenment and hope. The Reformation which, despite its tragic consequence in dividing Christendom, liberated Catholics and Protestants alike from fear and superstition, sprang from a new appraisal of the nature and destiny of men based on the Word of God as revealed in the Old and New Testaments. So too in the Evangelical Revival in eighteenth-century England and in the renewal of the German Church in its defiance of Hitler, it was by returning to the scriptural foundations that dry bones were made to live again. As the writer of the epistle to the Hebrews declares: 'The word of God is alive and active ... It sifts the thoughts and purposes of the heart.'[2] The Bible is a living force and not a dead letter.

There is enough diversity in the ways by which God has spoken to his people in past times, ranging from direct summons to service as in the lives of Abraham, Moses, Isaiah, Jeremiah, St. Paul, St. Augustine, St. Francis, to his less spectacular challenge to political and social reformers in the modern world, for us to be wary of expecting his Spirit to follow any predictable pattern. Jesus compared the effect of the Spirit with the vagaries of the wind, which blows where it wills,[3] and as Samuel discovered, 'men judge by appearances but the Lord judges by the heart'.[4] In the striking story in the book of Genesis of the blessing of the sons of Joseph by his old father Jacob on his deathbed,[5] the aged patriarch to his son's annoyance crossed his hands and laid the right hand of blessing upon the head of Joseph's younger boy instead of on the head of the elder boy as Joseph, and everyone else, expected.

But, as the parable suggests, the old man knew very well what he was doing. So, the Bible says to us, we cannot pin God down. It could be that we may have something to learn from the *Thoughts of Chairman Mao*, who is no more unlikely a channel of God's Spirit than Cyrus the Persian was to Isaiah's dejected and sceptical countrymen in exile in Babylon.[6] Who in the heyday of Pope Leo X, the acknowledged Vicar of Christ on earth, would have dared to suggest that a renegade monk, Martin Luther, son of a Saxon miner, could rock the Establishment and sponsor the beginning of a new era? God crossed his hands when Caiaphas confronted Jesus, as he did when John Wesley infuriated West Country rectors by claiming that the world was his parish or, for Protestants at least, when Pope John XXIII opened his arms to welcome his separated brethren.

The unequivocal witness of the Bible is that God over-rules the best-laid plans not only of his enemies but of his servants. St. Paul found this out to his dismay on more than one occasion;[7] as Moses had done in his day as well.[8] Isaiah's hope of a massive and triumphal return of the exiles to Jerusalem and of the ingathering of the scattered tribes of Israel to the Holy City was not fulfilled.[9] But in the providence of God St. Paul was guided away from Bithynia to preach the gospel in Macedonia and ultimately in Rome; the Israelites eventually reached the Promised Land despite the frustration of Moses' plans; and Jerusalem was destined to play a greater role than Isaiah had envisaged.

So it has been and will no doubt be again. The form of the Church as we have shaped it may not be the Church as God has planned it. But that there will always be a People of God to witness for him in the world is the theme of the whole Bible. What we ought to be doing now is not lamenting the decline of the Church as we have known it but keeping our minds open to receive what guidance God may be giving us and listening to whatever message he may have for us even if this comes from the most unexpected quarters, and through most unlikely messengers.

Herbert Butterfield has commended to us what he calls

the 'Abrahamic presupposition' as being the main requirement for any Christian. He is referring to the attitude of Abraham as defined by the author of the epistle to the Hebrews when he describes the patriarch leaving Ur of the Chaldees and going forward into the unknown future trusting only in God. We must be like Abraham, says Butterfield, who 'left home without knowing where he was to go'.[10] Old and cherished practices and traditions may have gone forever in the general shaking of the foundations which we are living through. We do not need to sit at the roadside, like Eli, with our hearts trembling for the ark of God.[11] This is God's world and the future is in his hands. We have to learn that the only certainty is Christ—and the whole Bible focuses our attention on him. Whether, like Timothy, we have been familiar with the scriptures from early childhood, they have as St. Paul said to him in his letter 'power to make you wise and lead you to salvation through faith in Christ Jesus'.[12]

But how can we best read the Bible? The simplest answer would seem to be to begin at the beginning and read straight through to the end. This is obviously one way, but it is not necessarily the best. The New English Bible and the Jerusalem Bible each run to a formidable total of almost two thousand pages, more than half of which are devoted to the Old Testament. We may be tempted to echo the comment of the Chinese pastor who said that 'reading the Old Testament is like eating a large crab; it turns out to be mostly shell with very little meat in it'. Many will feel that the late Bishop Wilson of Birmingham gave good advice to the soldiers who came to him in the Japanese prison camp where they were interned during the last war. The troops had run out of cigarette paper and the question put to the bishop was whether it would be sacrilege to use the thin paper of a Bible for that purpose. The bishop's understanding reply was: 'Begin with Leviticus!'

There is no single or simple answer to the question as

to how we should set about getting to know the Bible
better. Much depends on the type of mind we have and
the time we have at our disposal. Many have acquired the
habit of daily Bible reading, using the excellent booklets
of such organisations as the Bible Reading Fellowship[13]
and the International Bible Reading Association,[14]
which normally provide explanatory notes on the passage
prescribed for the day. Other people prefer to follow one
or other of the lectionaries recommended by the branch
of the Church to which they belong. Others again find it
more helpful to read a book of the Bible straight through
at a sitting.

Two suggestions are, however, perhaps worth making
at this point. One is that despite the inestimable advantage
of being able now to read the whole Bible in modern
English, it is still not an easy book to understand without
some accompanying explanation. In this respect the notes
provided in the margin of the Jerusalem Bible give it an
advantage over the New English Bible. Lack of space,
however, limits even the Jerusalem Bible in its attempt to
include both the text of the Bible and explanatory notes
at the same time. The second suggestion would be that to
avoid the danger of failing to see the wood for the trees, a
preliminary to any study of particular parts of the Bible
must be to become aware of the message of the Bible as a
whole.

I have tried to meet this second problem for the ordinary reader in my book: *The Bible Story*.[15] We may look
at the Bible as a pageant or a drama and rightly so, for it
is both. But it is basically a story, the story from Genesis
to Revelation of what God has done and is still doing to
show us the meaning of life, our place in the universe and
our hope for the future. Any particular book or passage
of the Old Testament that we may read and think about
should be seen as merely a part of the whole story. I have
also tried, and again for the ordinary reader, to provide
in my *One Volume Bible Commentary*[16] a companion to
Bible-reading which seeks to explain the contents of the

Bible as a whole and to bring out the themes and patterns which make the Bible one book from Genesis to Revelation in a way which can be understood in the twentieth century. Any who would like to have brief introductions describing how the Bible came into being and the background from which it sprang might be helped by my two paperbacks: 'The Plain Man looks at the Bible'[17] and The Rediscovery of the Bible.[18]

There has been in recent years a welcome flow of commentaries on individual books of the Bible ranging from the simpler approach of the Cambridge commentaries on the New English Bible[19] to more advanced series like the Torch Commentaries,[20] the new Clarendon[21] and Century[22] Bibles and Black's New Testament Commentaries.[23] Some of these series are not yet complete but there is now plenty of assistance available, providing an opportunity for all who wish to study the Bible seriously to acquaint themselves with the results of modern biblical scholarship presented in an interesting and readable way. In the sophisticated society of the Western world the time is long past when it was enough to hand the enquirer a copy of the Authorised Version and urge him to read it. Many will always cherish the Authorised Version for the unsurpassable beauty of its language, but as the Ethiopian official who was trying to understand the equivalent of the Authorised Version in his own day said to Philip the evangelist: How can I understand this unless someone guides me?[24]

It is unthinkable that the present tendency to relegate the Bible to limbo, or to bracket it with the myths, legends and sagas of the ancient world will continue for long. We should perhaps nowadays be inclined to qualify Tertullian's dictum that the soul of man is naturally Christian, since we have a greater understanding of the value of the other great world religions in their own right. But Christianity would take sides with other religions in claiming that there is 'a God-shaped cavity in every human heart'. Western materialism with its idolatrous worship of technological progress has blinded us all to this truth in varying measure. But it is a passing phase. The spirit of man, made in the image of God, has need of more than bigger and better gadgets, faster and safer travel or even the conquest of space.

It is not simply pious jargon but inescapable truth that we all have immortal longings in us. Unlike the other animals, who are also God's creatures, we are not ultimately satisfied if we have enough food and adequate shelter. Nor even in human terms does social status, realised ambition, or assured wealth seem to guarantee happiness or even contentment. There is no evidence that in the affluent societies of the West there is to be found, as we had been led to expect, a greater degree of job-satisfaction, a more productive use of leisure time, a more successful way of bringing up children, a greater expertise in devising the instruments of a more equitable and compassionate community. And too many of us still insist, in terms of the underprivileged Third World: Am I my brother's keeper?[25]

We have been bedevilled in recent years with the fallacy that 'the facts of life' are wholly concerned with sex. No-one in his senses would deny that sex is one of these facts. But there are others. Not the least of them is death. What do we say to the mother who has lost a child in an accident on the roads or in the air? What do we say if, despite the splendid technique of modern medicine, a teenage boy or girl is the victim of some incurable disease? There is there, except in a few cases, just sheer tragedy—no heroism, no inspiration and apparently no sense. Death makes sense only if we accept the message of the New Testament that our life here on earth is a pilgrimage and a preparation for a richer and fuller experience than anything we can even dream of.

NOTES

[1] John 10: 10
[2] Heb. 4: 12 f. N.E.B.
[3] John 3: 8 N.E.B.
[4] 1 Sam. 16: 7 N.E.B.

[5] Gen. 48: 1 ff.
[6] Isa. 45: 1 ff.
[7] Acts 16: 6 ff.
[8] Num. 20: 14 ff.
[9] Isa. 49: 8 ff.
[10] Heb. 11: 8 N.E.B.
[11] 1 Sam. 4: 13
[12] 2 Tim. 3: 15 N.E.B.
[13] 148, Buckingham Palace Road, London S.W.1.
[14] Robert Denholm House, Nutfield, Redhill, Surrey
[15] Collins (1971)
[16] Hodder and Stoughton (2nd impression 1969)
[17] Collins (6th impression 1965)
[18] Hodder and Stoughton (2nd edition: 2nd impression 1962)
[19] Cambridge University Press
[20] S.C.M. Press
[21] Oxford University Press
[22] Nelson and Oliphants
[23] A. & C. Black
[24] Acts 8: 26 ff.
[25] Gen. 4: 9